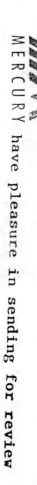

MERCURY have pleasure in sending for review

I'LL BE OVER IN THE MORNING

JAMES PILDITCH

£12.95

Publication date: 25 October 1990

Gold Arrow Publications Limited
862 Garratt Lane, London SW17 0NB
Tel: 081-682 3858   Fax: 081-682 3859

FOR FURTHER INFORMATION PLEASE CONTACT GOLD ARROW. IT IS REQUESTED THAT NO REVIEW APPEARS BEFORE PUBLICATION DATE. A CUTTING OF THE REVIEW WOULD BE APPRECIATED.

I'll be Over in the Morning

By the same author

The Silent Salesman
The Business of Product Design (with Douglas Scott)
Communication by Design
Talk about Design
Winning Ways

James Pilditch, CBE

I'll be Over in the Morning

A Practical Guide to Winning Business in Other Countries

Illustrated by the author

MERCURY

First published in 1990
by Mercury Books,
Gold Arrow Publications Limited,
862 Garratt Lane, London SW17 0NB

Set in Sabon by Phoenix Photosetting, Chatham, Kent
Printed and bound in Great Britain by
Mackays of Chatham PLC, Chatham, Kent

British Library Cataloguing in Publication Data
Pilditch, James
  I'll be over in the morning.
  1. International marketing
  I. Title
  658.848

ISBN 1–85251–034–X

Contents

Acknowledgements

A number of British design firms, as well as many other consultancy companies, have built substantial businesses in other countries. Writing about my own experiences takes nothing from them; indeed, aware of the difficulties, I acknowledge them now with honour.

My last book was criticized for having too little of me in it. This has too much. Remember, throughout, that most of the work described in this book was done by others. I remember it, and think of them with affection and gratitude. Allow me to thank, especially, Peter Cree, who kindly read the draft, confirmed facts and suggested many improvements. My debt to him, over many years, is incalculable. May I also thank friends and former colleagues who added stories from their own experience: Geoff Gibbons, Bill Goodenough, Jan Stael von Holstein and Kevin McGurk. Martin van Mesdag read the original outline and gave good advice. I thank him and Robert Postema, my courageous publisher, and Melanie O'Hara, who, perhaps no less bravely, typed the lot. To Anne, my wife, whose understanding and forebearance has been terribly tested, I offer special appreciation.

James Pilditch

Preface

Why this book? Why now? A stream of events tell us that more and more companies will want to work abroad, some for the first time. 1992, less a date than a symbol of a lasting movement to forge one huge market from Copenhagen to Capri, Leith to Lisbon, is the immediate provocation. But there are others. All business is becoming international. Big companies know that well; others have to come to terms with it. Or maybe they hope the gale of international business will rage over their heads. Not a chance. Even if you take a passive view, to defend what you've got (the first priority always), you have to think internationally. I write with certainty. My company won many competitive struggles in Britain because clients liked our international experience. Put it another way: local competitors lost business in their home market because they were not as internationally minded.

But international business is not easy. So how do you learn how to do it? Where do you start? This book tries to offer some answers. But it is far from a textbook; it tells how one firm did it. Without any pretensions to being right, it recounts how one small design office, started in London, grew to become perhaps the largest and most international of its kind in the world.

Believing we learn more from failure than success, I've been frank. The book is full of things we did wrong. The hope is that you will at least pick up some mistakes to avoid.

When he heard this book was being written, my friend and colleague for many years, Kevin McGurk, said it should be called 'Lies, Damned Lies and Case Histories'. But I've not written it that way. Case histories are marvels of tidiness. One step follows another in perfect sequence. You read them and say to yourself, 'my firm's not like that, we couldn't do the same'. The truth, I suspect, is that most firms are more like yours and mine than we're led to believe. The order in case histories, or in scientific experiments, dare I say, comes later, when they're published. Just as any development is likely to be a muddly affair of fits and starts, success and setback, so too is building an international business. Having said that, you do need a sense of purpose, a vision, neither inflexible as steel nor bendy as rubber, but one that keeps you straight whatever winds blow. I'll come to that.

I went on an international marketing course at INSEAD, the French business school. One day a Canadian lecturer was leading a case history about setting up a distribution system for a tyre company in Germany. He filled the blackboard with figures. It all sounded sensible to me. But then a Yorkshireman, high up in the back row of the lecture theatre cried out, 'You can't do that.' Startled, the lecturer asked, 'Why not?' 'Because,' retorted the Yorkshireman, 'those booggers are so crooked that when they die they don't bury them, they screw them into the ground.' To his credit, the lecturer wiped the board clean and said, 'OK, so what do you do?'

That is the spirit of this book: OK, what do you do? There is a difference, in other words, between theory and practice.

Harold Macmillan once said, 'Exporting is fun.' When you make your way through chilly mornings to catch the first flight or, late at night, in some cheerless hotel room, you rehearse once more the presentation you're to make the next day, when you hang around airports day after day and arrive home exhausted, you may wonder whether he was right.

But then I remember how we pipped twelve US design offices to win a contract in New York. I smell anew the cod-liver-oil smell of wooden stairs in our first foreign office in Oslo (and see in my mind's eye the boss who stole all the money skidding around the corner when he glimpsed me sitting by a window in a restaurant). I think how carefully we planned our presentation to BP and how monumentally we got it wrong, and I remember how we didn't get an Italian job because, according to the client, my striped shirt 'showed signs of levity'. I think of all the marvellous people I've met around the world, clients who became firm friends. Above all I honour, with love, the many people in the firm who worked with such vigour and enthusiasm to build business across the world. Macmillan was right after all.

Telling what happened in real life to one firm, this book is divided into three parts. First is a necessary preamble that describes my firm and its strategy. The second part, the heart of the book, tells how, with a long-term vision but a cautious start, we advanced from one market to another. The remaining chapters draw lessons.

When I started the firm, in a friend's flat, there was a record I played all day. It was 'Damned Yankees'. One line in it goes 'The only way to do it is do it'. That's right; so let's get on.

1 The Start and the Vision

My wife and I, just returned to London after several years in Canada, are staying in a friend's flat in Kensington. I am working at his desk, cutting sheets of plastic into strips to make (the first) transparent package for golf balls. The client is Spalding. Without much money, no home, not knowing London as a place to work in, it was easy to be nervous about starting a business. But that record is playing:

> It's fine to be a genius of course
> But keep that old horse
> Before the cart
> First you gotta have heart.

Just as there may be, as Noel Coward said, potency in cheap music, so there can be succour in simple words.

Spalding were just over Putney Bridge. I'd go to see the managing director. He became curious to see our 'offices'. 'It's no trouble,' he'd say, 'I'll run you back, just have a glimpse and be on my way.' This called for enterprise. In Earl's Court Road I'd smack my head and say, 'Oh, lord, it's my wife's birthday. I must buy some flowers.' Or, stopped at a traffic light, I'd leap out crying, 'Someone's having a baby. I must go to St George's . . . better get some flowers . . .' That florist must have been happy.

My firm started like this. I'd get a brief from a client, then hurry to a cafe in Dover Street, Mayfair. There, John Beadle, my partner-to-be, would be waiting. It was all a bit surreptitious; John was employed by a design office next door (THM Partners). Sipping frothy coffee from glass cups, unpalatable but popular at the time, I would outline that task. John did the work in the evenings freelance. I'd pick it up, then present it to the client.

James Brian Quinn, a professor of Business Administration at Dartmouth College in the United States, said one hallmark of successful companies is that they 'keep early costs low'. We did that, sure enough. Then, after a few months, John gave up his job to join me full-time. We were committed.

From the start, I can say, we got three things right. First, we had a clear idea of how we would divide responsibilities. John, a sensitive designer, would look after the creative work. Though knowing little about it, I would look after the business-getting and admin. We were partners. Each would have his say about everything, but if we disagreed, the one with the responsibility would decide the issue. That clarity was vital. It worked well.

Second, we had a budget. At that time design offices were thought unworldly, vague about money. I thought this an obstacle to getting business. So we told clients not only how we arrived at our estimates of fees, but what profit we aimed at (20 per cent). That reassured them.

Third, and central to this book, we had a vision. From the beginning, we intended to build a large, multidisciplinary and international design firm. It must have seemed absurd before we had any designers, a secretary or even an office, but the point is so important it is worth dwelling on. You've got to start with a vision. It is hard to hit goals if you don't know where they are.

My analysis, coloured no doubt by experience I'd had in an American design office, was this: business in Europe was bound to grow; companies would have to be bigger to compete; mergers were certain. To provide them with the services they'd need, we'd have to be a large-scale operation. In Amsterdam I angered a large audience of designers by arguing this. We all wanted more good design in the world, I said. But, in ones or twos, we wouldn't change much. If we wanted to change things, we'd have to go for the big firms. To do that, we'd need the resources big companies want. It is also true, as I learnt later, that people in big companies feel more comfortable when they deal with structured companies. So, for us to have the size and collection of skills big companies want became a goal.

Business, too, was bound to become more international, I was sure of it. So we would need to be international too. We never did agree with King George V, who is supposed to have said 'Abroad is awful,' adding after a pause, 'I know, I've been there.'

Further, we thought clients would want a *range* of design skills. At that time, most offices offered one or another. Some designed packaging, others were interior designers or product designers. Others designed print, and so forth. One or two offered several services – Milner Gray and Sir Misha Black's Design Research Unit was the outstanding example – but most did not.

Range of services

Even if you intend to build a range of services, you have to start somewhere. For the first year or two we mainly designed packaging, because it is the fastest way into any market. Then we added corporate-identity work – if less analytical than it became later, it was corporate identity none the less.

A large step was to move into product design. We joined forces with Douglas Scott, one of the unsung heroes of British design. Products he'd designed were on permanent exhibition in the Museum of Modern Art in New York. He'd worked on the Routemaster bus, familiar in London, and many other products that have stood the test of time. Later we built an architectural division, then an audio-visual activity. We grew both organically and by such innovations.

Later still, we developed two interesting companies. One, built by Kevin McGurk into a dazzling success handling multi-million-dollar contracts for US companies, as well as for Swiss, Dutch, Belgian and British household-name firms, invented and developed new products systematically. The other created products on a licensing basis. This needs to be explained. Virtually all the work you will read about was done on a fee basis. That is, we were paid for the time it took to do the job. More than once we smarted because products we designed sold like wildfire and we received no reward apart from our hourly fee. To do something about this, the new company worked for royalties. One range of products it developed for Marks & Spencer had sales in a test market of £55 million. So it was a good idea.

It is important to add that more and more of our work was based on information. We set up an information department, brilliantly run by Megan Thomas, rumoured to have come from MI5. Designers at first pooh-poohed this, fearing that it would somehow hamper their creativity, but they came to rely on it.

By the time we went public in 1980 our design skills included packaging, corporate identity, store planning (developed from the architectural division), product design (Scott left after a few years but the service continued to build) and new product development. We then acquired a number of excellent market-research companies, two micro-electronic companies, a financial-services company and others. The biggest acquisition was a design company in California.

Our philosophy was that we would 'get big by staying small'. Responsibility was devolved to people handling the business. That was true of companies and it was true of units within companies. The head of product design ran his business, as did the others. This way, the drive of dozens of people was fully engaged. Even when we reached the stage of having a revenue of over £20 million, sixteen companies and offices in several cities, there were only five of us in the centre.

At an early stage Peter Cree joined the firm and thanks to him we managed the company safely. Peter came from the Royal Navy where he'd been a navigator. By and large, ships in the Royal Navy don't bump into each other. Through all storms and travails, they arrive on time. That reliability and care is just what I needed. Peter was very thorough and accurate. He was cautious, seeing that the first duty of a business is to survive. With his background, I was sure he would be good with people. I've always looked for people who had proved they could set themselves an objective and achieve it. Before leaving the navy, Peter studied for the British Institute of Management exams and passed them, which must have taken determination. All this proved true. For many years managing director, he also became a superb business getter and builder. Thanks to Peter, we managed the company safely from a very early stage.

Our financial sysems were often admired by our clients. Curiously, in the design profession there was the widespread belief that good designers were bad at money, and, conversely, that if you were good at money you couldn't be much of a designer. That attitude has died now. By dividing responsibilities, at first simply, then in more elaborate ways, we tried to excel in both, managing excellent design well.

Spread risk

No less important, we spread our risk in three ways. First, we developed a range of services. Second, we worked with a number of markets (the story of this book). Third, we worked in a range of industries.

This last started simply. Naturally, we worked for firms wherever we could. But then we asked ourselves which were likely to be the growth industries of the future. After study, we picked maybe seven main industries. The financial world was one. Leisure was another. Retailing a third. Then, as you will see, we worked our way into them. Our idea was to stop being blown wherever the wind blew, but to go where the growth was. That was how we came to work for banks in eight countries, for several of the largest retailers in Britain, and so forth. Better still, into each we sold multiple services. The financial world we'd identified is an example: for banks and insurance companies we designed branches and offices, corporate identities, print matter, made audio-visual programmes, and did extensive market research.

We became a 'customer-focused' business. There is everything to be said for this. First, as customers' needs change so do you. (People who focus on their skills do well while those skills are wanted but, looking the wrong way, they often don't see changes in the market which render their abilities obsolete.) Second, as this book shows again and again, what clients like most is someone who understands their business. They are right. If you understand their business, you are more likely to be able to solve their problems. Third, it is easier, by and large, to sell a new service to an existing client than an existing service to a new client. That, alone, makes international business difficult. However, when you think of the benefits, which include what you learn and how much better you are able to serve clients wherever they are, the voyage is more than worthwhile.

Drive forward

Our defensive policy of spreading the risk, was matched by the aggressive policy of pushing out, always, for more business. We learnt the need for that in our first year. Metal Box gave us a job which more than doubled our revenue. It was to design packaging for British Home Stores, work which grew and grew for twelve years. John Beadle said, 'Thank goodness, that means we won't have to sell any more.' 'On the contrary,' I replied, 'we need to get their share of our business down.' I remembered a story current in Canada when I worked there. Woolworth had a bad name. It was said they would retain a design firm, giving them more and more work until they were wholly dependent on them, then they'd cut their prices in half. We didn't want that. Our rule became that no client would account for more than 20 per cent of our income.

That is one reason why we always sold vigorously. How we did it, and what we learnt, is described later. Peter Cree lists a few virtues of selling: it helps you control your destiny; it keeps your mind out, on the market, where it should be; and it is wonderful training.

What this preamble may reveal is that we started with a vision and the planning was good. But, as Tom Peters (author with Bob Waterman of *In Search of Excellence*) says, 'Plans don't achieve results, people do.' The company was blessed with many highly committed men and women who worked all hours, pouring their hearts into satisfying their customers by doing excellent work and providing remarkable service. To succeed internationally all those are necessary. Nine-to-five won't do it.

Two other qualities are worth mentioning. The first is integrity. Without sounding pious, I am sure that only by acting honestly, in the client's interest, can you build the sound reputation that encourages good firms to trust you. Apart from being the way to live, it makes good business sense. In New York one man I knew used to fleece people in St Louis because there was always Duluth or Des Moines or Minneapolis or a hundred other cities, but the quack medicine approach, never honourable, is not even effective any more. The world is smaller than we think. Often when we've tried to sell to new clients in one country they have telephoned previous clients of ours in another country for a reference.

Integrity runs all through a good business, and in time people outside get to know it.

The second quality you need to work internationally is persistence. Once I was thinking of hiring someone. I asked my neighbour – a lean, tough, Scottish colonel who had fought through jungles, in deserts and a dozen places besides – what qualities to look for. 'Stickability,' he said. By that he meant the ability to 'stay there', to keep at it. Every counsellor you ever meet in embassies abroad will tell you this is the single most important quality: the main reason why companies do not succeed in other markets is that they do not stick at it. They come in, try for a bit, then depart. The people in my firm who succeeded in building substantial business in other countries had 'stickability' in abundance: Eric Baskerville in the Netherlands, Philippe Rasquinet in Belgium and Jeremy Danks in Germany, amongst others.

International strategy

There were four strands to our international policy. One, start small, learning on a scale that wouldn't hurt us if it went wrong. Two, for many years Europe was our target and Germany the ultimate goal. But we wouldn't go straight to Germany. It was too big, advanced and unknown to us. We decided to build experience in other countries so that the day would come when German firms would accept that we had sufficient resources and international experience to be useful to them. We'd only sell in Germany when we were good and ready. Three, we'd do what we could do, one step at a time. Four, if opportunities came up, we'd take them, as long as they didn't divert us from our main, European aims. For example, although we worked in the Middle East quite a lot, we never saw it as part of our plan and never invested in it.

Why did we not put the Gulf among our priorities, even though it was, at the time, cascading money? I think there are three reasons. First, for some reason, right or wrong, I never saw it as a long-term market, one to persevere in. Second, we didn't know much about it. The cost of learning, we thought, would be high. Third, we tried to do high-quality work, to make a profit, and to enjoy ourselves. One of these, we feared, would be lacking.

Later our horizons grew. We developed a global strategy, our own 'triad'. Europe was our home market. The United States was a vast market we had to be in, and South-east Asia was what we called 'the golden tomorrow'. It all happened.

2 Short Steps: Eire and Scotland

The office had been going maybe a year. I had a secretary in my room and two designers in a studio next door. This girl walked in. She wanted a job. Today I'd have no trouble saying she was from Singapore or Malaya. But then I had no idea where she was from. She took my breath away, and not only mine. She was stunning. As I was looking at her portfolio, the phone rang. It was Neil Shakery, one of the designers. 'Hire her,' he commanded. A moment later my secretary gave me a note from Geoff Woollard, the other designer. 'Yes,' it said simply. But I couldn't; we just didn't have a job for her. As she left I said how sorry I was we couldn't employ her. 'It's because I'm a woman,' she said and sighed at the inequity of it all. 'Honey,' I replied, putting my arm around her, 'don't ever change a thing.'

I have always tried to right the unfairness she felt, but the point of the story is how ignorant we were of the world. The Far East, South-east Asia, and many places closer, could have been on the moon for all we knew or cared. Our horizons were nearer. By then our offices, a yawning, rent-gobbling 500-square feet, were in Gloucester Place, no distance from Baker Street. Business was coming in quite well – a beer can for Simonds, an overall identity for a chain of wool shops, and more. When I say business came in, I mean I went to find it. That's important. When we started, I thought having a design office would be like having a shop: at first you'd have to find the customers, but after a while they'd find you. You'd just sit there, soon the doorbell would tinkle. While, as you grow, there is a great deal of 'repeat' business, it doesn't work like that. Although one day it did. A man walked into our office one wet evening, his arms full of packages. He dropped them on a desk and went downstairs for more. I peeked out of the rain-streaked window. He was rummaging in the boot of a white Rolls-Royce. Then he was back. He wanted us, he said without preamble, to redesign them all, maybe a hundred packages. At any time this is a good job. In those days it was heady.

'We'd love to do the work,' I said, 'but we may not be able to.' His packages were all for baby products. We were working on baby products for Johnson & Johnson. I called the marketing manager at J&J. Would he mind if we took on this job? He'd rather we didn't he replied. So we didn't. Even though we had no contractual arrangement with J&J, and they promised us nothing, we accepted the morality without question. It was too bad.

This man walked in with 100 packages

This self-imposed ordinance, that we wouldn't work for the competitor of any client, soon became difficult. What if a firm making baby products in another country approached us? Would that be all right? If we worked for one company in a large group, did that prevent us from working for any company in a competitive group? If we worked for Debenhams (as we did in a large way), would that stop us working for House of Fraser (we later handled all the design of £100 million refurbishment programme)? Our attitude, when the question arose, was that we wouldn't work for both at the same time. But even that restraint is tricky. Later we worked for ITT companies in a wide range of industries in eight countries. Did that mean we couldn't work for any of their competitors in any country? For a long time those were the sort of standards we held. Determined not to betray our clients' trust, we worried endlessly about this. In the end, we came to think we'd been harsh with ourselves. Much of the problem went away. In some cases the question is vital, in others less so. Many clients, we discovered, don't mind. Some feel they have no right to restrain our trade. Others, providing they know you will honour their confidences, welcome the wider experience you gain of their industry. In any event, we always built our own 'Chinese walls', so that work was handled by people in different teams.

To Eire

The scale of those problems lay in the future. Here were we, in England, growing, ploughing back, doing all right. But we *did* have our larger goal. Perhaps it doesn't count as international, but to us Ireland seemed foreign enough. On the principle of starting small, taking small steps, that is where we first ventured.

It came about through Alec Crichton, then Governor of the Bank of Ireland and director of Jameson, the distillery. He had the idea of developing a superior Irish whiskey, one that had lain in the cask longer than usual. He asked us to design a new bottle as well as the label, carton and supporting promotion bits. That struck us as extravagant. We searched the glass industry in Britain and found a suitable stock bottle already in production. It worked beautifully and saved Jameson a lot of money. Crichton liked that attitude. He gave us more work and introduced us to Don Carroll, who owned Carroll's tobacco firm. Under John Beadle's guidance, one of our designers, John Harris, designed one brand leader after another. He was remarkably successful.

All plain sailing. We'd stay at the Shelborne in Dublin, loving the slightly raffish, horsey gentry who patronized the bar. We admired the elegant squares of Dublin, ate well, worked easily. Only when we started to work in Cork did we begin to learn the perils of doing business in another country.

Early lessons

The Irish Development Agency (IDA), had seen our work; indeed, I'd been to see them a number of times. They introduced us to Mitchelstown Creameries, and had a scheme which even subsidized our fees. Mitchelstown was an amalgam of local dairies, all too small to compete on any big stage. Admiring Kerrygold, who'd developed one brand name for their diverse range, they wanted to do the same. That was fine. I took the brief. Already it was my habit to write notes on the trip home, have them typed first thing next morning and sent off that day.

When I went back to Mitchelstown with the work after a week or two they didn't want what we'd done. 'But, but,' I blustered, 'this is what you said,' waving my notes in front of them. 'Oh yes,' they agreed, 'but we've had a little think.' From that I learned to check every decision with every person individually in the room. We invariably sent meeting notes rapidly, with a reminder that they were what we would work to. From Mitchelstown on, we learnt to make it clear in estimates that if clients altered their brief, we'd charge more for extra work.

In Dublin I had an embarrassing experience. I'd been to lunch in a brand new restaurant, the last word. In the evening John Lepere, the marketing director of Carroll's, and his wife picked me up to go to dinner. 'We're going somewhere new,' they said, obviously excited. As we drove along I recognized a scene here, another there. It dawned on me: this is where I'd had lunch. Should I say? The mood was such that it would surely spoil their pleasure. I kept quiet: it would be all right. But as we walked in the door the *maître d'hôtel* beamed at me and said, 'And you here at lunchtime too. How nice of you to bring your friends so soon.' It spoilt that evening, but no more. We continued to work for John, and for a growing number of companies in Eire.

We also worked in Northern Ireland. In London we were handling a large programme for Charrington United Breweries, a brewery put together by E. P. Taylor, the Canadian millionaire. They had thousands of pubs, including a number in Belfast. I was sent there to meet the chairman of the Irish company, Sir Robin Kinahan. I arrived first thing. Clearly, it was a nuisance to him. 'My car's outside,' he said. 'Take it and visit some pubs. Come back for lunch. We'll talk then.' His car, a green Mercedes, was the largest I'd ever seen. A driver hovered, waiting to be told where to go. 'Take me to some pubs,' I said. We decided on a couple in the city, two in the suburbs and two in the country. I walked into the first one. Even at that early hour there were one or two patrons standing by the bar. They glowered at me. I had to buy a drink to take their eyes off me. Six of those, and by lunchtime I could hardly speak to Sir Robin or anyone else.

Multiple choice

In Ireland, too, we learnt a lasting lesson. John Beadle always believed that the professional way to work with clients was to present them with one solution, our answer to their problem. I'd always worried about that and, in later years, we proved it to be wrong. On one occasion, Peter Cree was managing a project for Ewart's, the Irish textile firm. They sent him to New York, to meet the company's people there. Peter showed the one solution. The Americans were quiet, unconvinced. 'Did you', they asked tentatively, 'develop any other ideas?' Peter had taken with him all the dozens of scribbles and sketches the designers had done to arrive at their answer. He went through them, explaining why each had been done and why it had been rejected by us. That convinced them. They saw the background and were amazed at the work that had gone into their project.

Service

Another lesson we picked up soon was this: in a busy office work for companies far away can easily be put to one side. From the earliest days we took the opposite tack. It was cardinal, we thought, to give our clients abroad exemplary service. We were often congratulated for it. Our reasoning was simple: doing work abroad is harder; if you don't concentrate on it there are many more chances for it to go wrong. Also, we were always conscious of coming from behind. For clients there is every reason to use designers who are local. They know the country better, they are easier to reach and they cost less. Partly, although not only, because we came from further away, our costs were higher. We had to demonstrate our superiority, yes, but a first step was to rub out any obvious, measurable, expected drawbacks. Service was one of them.

Mastering the problems of providing good service, or, to put it differently, daily insisting on good service from ourselves, driving ourselves that bit harder, was a lasting contribution to our international growth.

Scotland

To couple Scotland with international selling might sound exaggerated, but perhaps what made us see it this way was the flight. We weren't quite used to that, though I heard a fierce story from a friend at British Steel. From time to time the company lent its aircraft to Willie Ross, then Secretary of State for Scotland. My friend was earmarked to accompany him. Throughout the journey Willie Ross said nothing. As they were coming in to land in Glasgow he turned to my friend and barked, 'What's yerr name anyway?' My friend told

him. 'Aye,' said the secretary of state, as though fully satisfied. He
turned back to his papers. After a moment he looked up and added,
'And I didn't like yerr faither either.'

We met our first Scottish client at a party in London. Allan Graham ran his father's toy firm in north London. He asked me to see
him for lunch. He welcomed me perfunctorily and waved me to sit
down. 'We'll play a game,' he announced. 'I know the rules, I'll start.'
Between us, on his desk, was a sheet of paper, pencilled in squares.
He gave me a folded wedge of paper and took another for himself.
These were counters. For half an hour he threw a dice then moved the
counters. I hadn't any idea what was going on. Between moves, he'd
lean to his right and open a desk drawer. From it he took a small
blowpipe, looked at a small statuette of a knight in armour in a far
corner of the room and blew a pea at it. If the pea hit the knight's
shield, as it always did, the knight's sword clanked down.

After lunch Allan agreed to visit our offices. He brought a child's
carpentry set. He wanted the box redesigned. Geoff Woollard, a
sound designer who radiates integrity, opened the box thoughtfully
and took out a toy saw. To my horror, he bent it double. 'How', he

He blew peas at a statuette

asked, 'do you expect to sell this junk?' Allan, not surprisingly, was annoyed. He swept off. A year later he returned. 'Geoff was right,' he said. Allan had re-sourced the entire contents of the carpentry set to improve the standard. It was now very good. Geoff redesigned the package, treating carpentry less as jolly fun than as a serious craft. It sold famously for years.

During that year Allan moved his company to Scotland, taking advantage of a bountiful government scheme. Marvellous at golf and at shooting, he'd jumped at the offer. His company used us to design one product and package after another. Each time, sales tripled or quadrupled. And, as the reputation for quality spread, success begat success.

We worked with Allan to put more form in his product range, reducing it from fifty-two items in one shopping list, to thirteen or fourteen grouped in four discrete business areas. There is more to design than design, we were learning. Together we developed a range of 'serious' products – chemistry sets, a microscope and others. They all had three virtues: they were of good quality (the days of buying plastic junk from Hong Kong were over); they were exclusive (these two virtues pushed up the added-value); and they were not fashion items, with a short, even one-Christmas, life. These toys, like Monopoly, went on and on.

More than design

Now we were developing ourselves, thinking how to improve Allan's business. People who say design is just about good looks miss the point. Though we expressed ourselves by design, I like to think of it as 'intelligence made visible'. Two examples illustrate our attitude.

The contractors who built the Bull Ring city centre in Birmingham were worried. People weren't going there; they weren't letting shops on the site. They asked us to design an attractive identity for it. Before designing anything we suggested they conduct market research to find *why* shoppers didn't go there. Results surprised us. To enter the Bull Ring on foot you had to go through tunnels – and people don't like tunnels. We suggested two steps: open the tunnels, and bring in a magnet – Marks & Spencer would have been ideal – to attract people; improve the 'product', in other words.

Our experience with London Transport can make the same point. John Stansby, a dear friend who became deputy chairman of London Transport, explained that the underground system was investing millions in development but none of it showed. He wanted us to design something or redo a couple of stations to show Londoners that their underground was changing. He gave us three stations to look at. We conducted a photo survey – often a good idea, because it is so truthful; you can see a cigarette butt at fifty paces. The day came when we were to present our recommendations to Stansby. To his dismay, we came with no elegant perspectives, indeed no design at all. Our recommendation was a three word sentence: clean the place. Using the photo survey we showed what we meant. The stations were filthy. Stansby agreed. He arranged a meeting of London Underground to start the process. They sent thirteen men, twelve from the unions. We sent one designer, Geoff Gibbons. The men just couldn't see the dirt or torn posters or decay. What we thought straightforward turned out to be insurmountable. One union was responsible for cleaning walls from the ground to as high as a brush would reach. Another looked after the tunnel and arched ceilings above that height. To clean an electric clock with advertising panels required the consent of three unions. So this is a good and a bad story. It is good to see design as more than decoration. It is bad to make recommendations that won't be implemented, and silly of us to send one designer, however experienced, into a meeting like that.

But I've drifted in space and time. London Underground is not in Scotland . . .

Our early and naïve attitude, that Scotland was far and different, faded. We worked for many companies there, some local, some as big as any. The most striking was the Royal Bank of Scotland. We worked for that distinguished company almost continuously for twenty years. Mark Woodhams designed the symbol and identity you now see. A few months after it was launched, the new symbol appeared in a cartoon in *The Scotsman*. It showed a 'late-night reveller' weaving his way down Sauchiehall Street in the early hours. He looks up at the bank's new symbol and says, 'Wha's happened to the bliddy clock?' This showed recognition, even affection.

Peter Cree, who managed the Royal Bank work, told that story 100 times, at every sales presentation he could. We groaned. But Peter was right. We so often change presentations because we tire of them, forgetting that new clients have never seen or heard them before. If you're doing something right, keep doing it.

3   First Office Abroad: Norway

When Ted Heath was prime minister, PA (now PA Consulting Group) were employed to seek the best site for a new town in the west of England. Michael Dineen, later a director of Extel, was the consultant chosen to look at one ancient seaside town. He visited companies newly installed there to ask why they had chosen it. He expected to hear about the availability of labour, or resources or communications or some other, sound, rational reason. Instead, in almost every case, the directors said, 'Well, you see, my daughter married a man down here and we thought we'd like to be near them' or, 'I've always been keen on sailing and it is wonderful here.' In other words, an astonishing number of answers were personal.

That may not always be the case, but our skein of reasons for going to Norway certainly had a personal strand. I'd fallen in love with Norway when, as a student, I hitch-hiked there one summer. The idea was to stay in youth hostels. The day the steamer from Newcastle arrived in Oslo every hostel in the country closed: it was the end of their season. I took a small boat north, then inland, criss-crossing the deep, black, still water of the Hardangerfjord. Rucksack on my back, I made my way up a dusty, snaking road to a high plateau, the Hardangervidda, where there was nothing but huge boulders strewn by God millions of years ago. I hitched east to Oslo, down the west coast of Sweden to Copenhagen then back to Norway, around the south coast.

Beyond Kristiansand an air-force ambulance gave me a lift. The driver was a doctor. We were bowling along through low, scrubby hills, miles from anywhere when the battery fell out of the car. We glided to a halt. There, on the road behind us, was the battery. 'Thank goodness you're here,' said the doctor, 'I know nothing about cars.' Neither, sadly, do I. We sat on the running board of the ambulance looking at the empty hills. We'd still be there except that within ten minutes, from heaven knows where, a man rode up on a bicycle. He was an electrician. A miracle. Off we went, first to the doctor's camp, Spitfires on the runway, then to his home. After three days I was still there, searching for excuses to escape his generous hospitality.

So it always was. One Norwegian let me sleep on the floor of his electrical shop. Another cleared the top of his chopping table at the back of his butcher's shop, where I slept with great sausages hanging above me. Everywhere, people were embarrassingly kind. The warmth of the people, their rectitude and reticence, their remembrance of Britain's part in the war, affected me no less than the pale beauty of Norway.

Sleeping on a butcher's table

Small wonder that when a giant of a Norwegian, Anthon B. Nilsson, came to the office, I was easy to persuade. A general who had become a management consultant, he was convinced that design was needed in Norway. It would become important, he believed. He wanted to start a design office in Oslo, but needed our help.

Why Norway?

As well as suiting my sentiments, the rationale for us was easy to find.
We wanted to start small. Norway is a small country. People speak
English. Norway is on the periphery of Europe and that fitted in with
the rough concept we had in our minds of 'encircling' the great
markets of Europe. Our idea was to work our way in, a step at a time,
to the central target of Germany.

I also assumed that the general was a good administrator and, with
his consultancy experience, would have knowledge of and access to
good Norwegian companies.

Yes, we might just manage it; to plant our first foot abroad. We
formed a jointly owned company, our first overseas investment.
Nilsson brought his assistant into the company, an Irishman. They
opened an office near the American embassy in Oslo, and brought in
a couple of designers. Work came in slowly, but it came. Within a few
months the general just left. He decided it wasn't what he wanted. He
left his assistant in charge. I doubted the man's ability, but have
always hoped people will grow into the responsibilities they're given.
So we let it run. I used to go quite often, trying to help in various
ways, making sales calls with no great success. But business grew.

Karen Munck, a wonderful designer in our London office who, by
coincidence, had a Norwegian background, went over for some
months. So did Clive Barron, a designer now practising in Manchester. They were sophisticated designers, Karen the more experienced
of the two. They found themselves in a design climate that was
innocent and conventional. It was in Norway, perhaps, that I first
learnt to put down my glass and steal away whenever a group of
designers start asking, 'What do we mean by design, anyway?' You
know you are in for a long, inconclusive evening.

At a party in Oslo one evening a designer stated, as an elementary
confirmation of the laws of nature, that chairs are made of wood.
Any ethical designer would only use wood, that was obvious. 'But
why?' asked Karen. 'What's wrong with metal? Or glass? Or plas-
tics? Or' – getting carried away – 'cardboard?' The Norwegians were
incredulous. To me it was a demonstration of the difference between
the craft tradition, from which Norwegian design has grown, and the
industrial tradition, from which the bulk of British and American
design evolved. It showed, too, the open-mindedness of the good
designer, mentally free to challenge any dogma.

Money started to go wrong, for the obvious reason: we had higher
costs than revenue. The Irishman wasn't bringing in the business.

One day I learnt he had raided the till, emptied the remaining bank account and disappeared. He's the fellow I saw ducking around the corner some weeks later and have never seen or heard of since. Happily, we lost little money. No harm had been done. That was the sense of starting small where it didn't much matter. Karen and Clive came home, Karen staying in the firm in London for years, producing many outstanding designs.

Our manager ducked around the corner

Reading the story now it is easy to spot things we did wrong. We didn't neglect the office. That wasn't a fault. What mistakes did we make? It might interest you to write down what you think.

It would have been easy to keep that firm in Oslo. My soft spot was soft as ever, but we were beginning to feel that if we were going to be in Scandinavia, we should be in the heart of it.

4 Bigger, Better: Sweden

Sooner or later we'd have to be in Sweden, Norway's big neighbour. We knew nothing about it other than being overawed by its reputation for social progress and prosperity. I asked around – in Norway, at the Design Council, the Department of Industry, and wherever I could. No one knew very much, although the names of a number of individual designer-craftsmen came up. One office that impressed me was that of Sigvard Bernadotte, which did serious product design: typewriters and calculating machines (for FACIT) and many others. Count Sigvard Bernadotte's great grand-mother was Queen Victoria, his mother the daughter of the Duke of Connaught. His father was the reigning King of Sweden. Although Sigvard had renounced the title of prince (he now wants it back), he was no dilettante. His designs for Georg Jensen were well-known, and behind him was a sound office with extremely able product designers.

We looked carefully. The timing for an approach might be right, too. Sigvard had just ended a long partnership with Acton Bjorn, a famous Danish designer. Maybe he needed company. Distinguished as he was, small as we were, we thought it worth a try. I went to see him in Stockholm. We met in his office in Master Samuelsgatan, then he took me to lunch at Operakällaren, a grand restaurant in the *belle époque* style. He sat with his back to the royal palace, visible across the water, a constant reminder of his heritage. My tentative proposal was that if we co-operated we could each be stronger. He'd be in a better position to work for the important international Swedish companies and together we could expand our presence in Scandinavia.

After a few meetings we formed a working relationship which developed excellently. We came to have shares in each other's company and later we acquired a majority in his company. We went to and fro all the time. We swapped information, leads, ideas and case histories. As far as we could, we introduced our financial and other management methods.

Sigvard was like a father or uncle to me and I enjoyed acting as his

ADC, smoothing his path. We all came to love him and very much enjoyed working with the people in his office, Hans Sjöholm, Peter Maddock, an Englishman, and others. To their product design we added graphics and started to sell the London services in Sweden, with great success. To these two services, we added a third we had practised in London, interior design. Jonas Tengbom, son of one of Sweden's famous architects, joined us and designed wonderful new offices for us overlooking the great, grey waters of Slussen.

With their good design, which spoke for itself, Sigvard's reputation, our window to the wider world and our selling and PR approach, things went well. Sigvard knew everyone and was admired universally. Reserved, shy and gentlemanly, he'd never push himself or even his office. To overcome that we helped the office set up systematic sales methods. The success was infectious.

From cars to buses

We were invited to dinner by the president of Saab, Kurt Mileikowsky. Half Russian, wholly fascinating, he was a distinguished scientist, prolific reader and visionary talker. He sent a company plane to Stockholm to fly us to the Saab plant. Over an elegant dinner Mileikowsky spoke about space travel. By the turn of the century, he prophesied, there would be 9,000 people living on the moon. One consequence of that evening was that we were appointed to design part of a new car, the front or the back, I don't remember. A funny way to do things.

Sigvard got us into StorStockholms Lokaltrafik, the Stockholm transport system. The system looked then, as it does now, dull and official and unimaginative. All the trams and buses were a dark maroon, dull in the grey light of a Swedish winter. After lots of study and design, we made a polished presentation. On slides we showed the vehicles in the streets, only now they were bright yellow. A secondary colour was blue. Blue and yellow are the Swedish colours, but that wasn't the reason for our choice. We wanted to make the buses and trams more visible, both from a safety point of view and to enliven the wintry streets. That was just one detail of the large amount of work we showed, but it was too much for the heavy, socialist bureaucrats who ran the system. Nothing came of it.

The design work by Mike Russell was excellent and his presentation marvellous, so I couldn't understand why it wasn't accepted. One factor may have been that Sigvard Bernadotte, the designer and I gave the presentation in English. In Sweden you assume everyone speaks English, but that is not always so, and this may have been such an occasion. Another reason may have been 'local preference', a factor we discovered when the Stockholm office got the job of designing the identity for a legislative district of the city. That came thanks to our work with the Labour-controlled London borough of Lewisham, an example of experience in one country helping to get business in another. (Red though they were, we had persuaded Lewisham to accept as their symbol and identity a gold crown on a blue background. One councillor asked 'What's wrong with the colour of London buses?' Another councillor – perhaps Mrs Callaghan, wife of the prime minister-to-be – interjected, 'We've paid to have experts. Why don't we listen to them?')

We did the designs for the Stockholm district from London. The client didn't like them. Our Swedish designers then put forward alternatives which to my eyes weren't a patch on ours, either practically or aesthetically. Still, the client preferred them and used them. This story shows that, whatever proponents of global marketing say (and I can be one of them), people in different countries can have different tastes. There's no getting away from it. Often work done in London by highly qualified and experienced designers is liked abroad, but not always. So what do you do then? If we are to be international, to say nothing of being successful, we must satisfy the tastes of our customers, not our own. Even on the mainland of Europe such differences occur. We were once asked to design a pan-European car radio for Schaub-Lorenz in Germany. They liked our design; their sister company in France disliked it. The subject is a subtle one. It even has moral and professional implications designers don't always accept.

To tell the truth, our graphic designers in Stockholm were by no means as experienced or sensitive as their colleagues in London. Indeed, hiring them was the first rent in our otherwise seamless partnership. The arrangement we had with Sigvard was that we recognized his superior knowledge of product design. At our request, he kept an eye on our product designers in London, and was involved in every appointment. Similarly, we took the lead in graphics. Should they hire graphic designers, it was understood, we would vet them. They forgot this side of the bargain. In Stockholm they hired, without telling us, an American designer whose experience had been confined to cosmetic packaging, insufficient experience in our view.

The case of Alfa-Laval illustrated the limitations of not sharing experience. The Swedish designers created the symbol and clumsy lettering you see now. Because they had none of the extensive knowledge we had acquired of developing corporate identities and its complexities, the need for sound implementation and, no less vital, good communications, they only knew enough to do a superficial job. As a result the Swedes got a job that lasted a few weeks instead of doing a better job for the client which could have led to two years' work. They sold a symbol; they didn't solve an international communications problem.

The principal of having leaders for each discipline, wherever the offices are, is a good one, but each local office wants to stand on its own feet. Reconciling that difference is not always easy. On one side there is the 'local preference' argument we saw with the Stockholm district. On the other, there is 'professional competence', with Alfa-Laval.

Marabou

The issue doesn't always arise. Through Sigvard Bernadotte our designers in London got a job with Marabou, the Swedish chocolate firm. It was a family business. The late Johan Throne-Holst was the chairman. His offices on the outskirts of Stockholm were an advanced example of 'Bürolandschaft' – open plan but with costly sound-absorbent ceilings and walls, and soft carpets. Movable screens were designed to break up open space, create small work areas, yet let everyone be together, encouraging easy contact between people. The chairman's own space was there, with everyone else. Even more remarkable, there were fine paintings everywhere. By this secretary was a Paul Klee. Over there was a Miró, perhaps a Matisse. They were not confined to the smart parts directors use – that in itself was telling. When you think how mean and bad most pictures are in most offices, you can imagine how inspiring this was.

Dazzled, I asked Throne-Holst what had led him to invest in paintings this way. He had learnt from his father, he said, who had owned the Freia chocolate factory in Oslo. During the first war he commissioned 'some local chap' to paint a mural in the staff canteen. The 'local chap' was Munch. 'Today,' Throne-Holst said with a smile, 'the mural is worth more than the factory.'

I have told this story to British businessmen who, by and large, think buying art is a misuse of company funds. Almost the only good pictures I've seen in a British company are in the headquarters of WH Smith and of British–American Tobacco. We did a lot of work for BAT. One day I was told the chairman, Sir Duncan Oppenheim, wanted to see me. 'Look at his pictures,' someone said. Sir Duncan had a large, panelled, rather sombre office. On his walls were pictures so famous I thought they must be copies. You see them everywhere. 'Oh, no,' my friend said later, 'they're the originals.' But Sir Duncan is a rare man and a painter of note himself.

By coincidence, the designer we assigned to the Marabou project was Karen Munck, who'd been in Oslo. Karen is one of the best graphic designers I've met – very imaginative, always to the point, truthful in her work as in her life. When briefing us, Throne-Holst insisted we keep the symbol the company had used for years. It was a bird, a marabou. We discovered the marabou is an East African scavenging bird, a mangy-looking creature. Karen didn't think it had much to do with chocolates; something warm and round and generous was more fitting. Karen re-designed the name that way. We'd seen a Marabou commercial in which an attractive Swedish actress opens a bar of chocolate and bites it, saying, 'Mmmmm – Marabou.' Karen made that her design: Mmmmm . . . Marabou. It was ideal. But what about the bird? Karen kept it on a few sketches, reduced to a small roundel. It was, as R. H. Wilenski would have said, 'a vestigial remnant', no more. 'What's that for?' asked Throne-Holst. 'We don't need that.'

Karen's whole programme was accepted with enthusiasm. From London, though, it was hard for us to provide at reasonable cost the mass of package design Marabou wanted. We did need local graphic designers. But that presented its own difficulties – designers often don't want to execute someone else's work. In their eyes it reduces their creative status.

Husqvarna

Husqvarna made cannons, but had diversified into lighter, consumer and other industrial products. Four or five of us from London studied the company and its markets. The president and directors liked the strategy we proposed and, weeks later, loved the design Mike Russell created for them. The advertising manager, so excited, wanted to tell his agency at once. 'Don't do it,' I warned; 'wait a day or two.' He ignored me and called the agency the day after we left. In no time they killed our design work and subsequently re-did it themselves. This had happened before (hence my warning) and since. Advertising agencies can look on designers as competitors, something I have never understood. That attitude is probably confined to smaller agencies. In Britain, the Netherlands, France, Germany, Belgium, for instance, we have been keen allies.

While the graphic side of the Stockholm office was growing, with the large programmes being handled in London, so did the product design. Product designers there designed earth-moving equipment for Volvo, a new concept of petrol station for Esso, the world's first visual telephone (you can see the person you're talking to) for Ericsson, and lots more. The interior side was moving too. Sometimes we co-operated across disciplines from country to country. When Jonas Tengbom redeveloped the Hotel Reisen, graphic designers in London created all the identity and visual material for it.

Perils of translation

We produced a poster-sized sheet that folded like a map, to show the spread of our international work. Once in a while we'd send a newsletter to clients and prospects in each country. Deliberately, it was neither glossy nor smart, but typewritten. We wanted it to be something you'd read in a moment, news you could deal with then and there. How often do you see glossy news-sheets that are so smart you carry them back and forth in your briefcase for days before finally throwing them away – unread?

One newsletter in Sweden alerted us to the perils of translation. We'd written it in English, then translated it into Swedish. Following the basic rule, the translation was done into the translators' native language. My wife, who is Swedish, and a Swedish friend, both of whom have lived in England for years and speak exquisite English, did it for us. Then we sent the text to Sigvard. He couldn't read it. It was gibberish.

Design, like everything else, is full of jargon which we don't even notice. So if you translate into other languages, you must have not just a native speaker but a translator who knows your business. And try it out on friends in your business in the country concerned before using it.

Sudden collapse

The whole thing was working, even across boundaries. The international network we had dreamed of was coming together. People moved back and forth from one office to another most days. Designers swapped about too. Peter Maddock, from Stockholm, worked for one or more firms in England, and Roger Ford, head of product design in London, spent time in Sweden.

Then, quite suddenly, after maybe five years, the Swedish office fell apart. Its success led directly to its failure. Because the office was very good, with household-name clients, undoubtedly the leading design office in the country, it is worth asking what went wrong? And how did we fail to put it right?

What happened was this: the Swedish office had a good year, made good profits. One part was losing money, but that is always the way with start-ups. Otherwise all was very good. Every person in the Stockholm office came to London for the weekend to celebrate their success. That was fun, until we learned that the company paid every penny. They blew the whole year's profit in one weekend.

At first we were staggered by their lack of financial prudence. But then we realized it wasn't imprudence but ignorance. They thought profit was what you could spend (forgetting, by the way, that over half the profit belonged to us). Our code was sterner. We always divided our profit three ways: tax, profit-share to staff, and plough-back into the business.

We thought it was a folly but not serious. We were wrong. With no cushion of carried-forward profits to rely on, a gap soon widened between money coming in and money going out. To cover it, Sigvard borrowed from the bank. Soon, for reasons I'm still not clear about, this successful company started making losses. It was an astonishing turn-round. The bank wanted more assurances. What should we do? We'd already invested a good deal, far more than any agreement called for. We did guarantee some and sent our financial director from London to go into the details. One person in the office was given financial authority and told to cut costs harshly. Several times I went to Stockholm. With the new management team I'd set up, I'd agree steps they should take. A week or two later I'd return – to see none had been taken. They were like rabbits caught in headlights, frozen. Recently I've read a book about the psychology of incompetence in war. Sometimes when facing a crisis, clever generals can be stilled into inactivity, immobile, unable to move. That seemed to be what happened here.

Morale fell, the firm started to crumble. The most loyal and able staff started planning how to start their own offices. In London we reached the stage, perhaps prematurely, when we thought we must stem the losses for our own sake. We paid all their bills and wound up the office. But Sigvard, my dear friend, was unreconciled. He understood the change no more than we did. As an example to others, we had waived all monies owing to us and, in return, I'd asked him to cut his pay for six months. That wounded him. To my infinite sadness, he never spoke to me again.

I dwell on this because the aim of this book is to help people to build their international business. In both Norway and Sweden we'd seen plants, carefully nurtured, wither. It should be instructive to ask why.

Wally Olins, who has built his own international corporate-identity business, once told me his office looked democratic, but wasn't. Our office, he said, didn't look democratic but it was, as Peter Cree confirmed. Our company in London was characterized by being democratic and devolved. Responsibility was given wholly to the people closest to the action. Designers and others were trusted with far more responsibility than you'd normally find. I like this, but Peter thought it could go too far. In the name of devolving responsibility and trusting people, we were sometimes lax. That may be part of the explanation of the Swedish case.

We worked hard at the Swedish office. The quality of their product design needed nothing from us. Their graphic design was not as good as ours, but no worse than the level in Sweden. That wasn't the problem. They had a wonderful reputation and sold with vigour. We had set up the financial systems and received monthly analyses. The appointment of the American designer, Sigvard's loan from the bank, and their decision to spend all the profit showed, though, that they decided some quite large matters without our knowledge. Notwithstanding the ownership, they felt independent. In a way I'd pushed that to discourage any idea that once they'd been bought they were no longer responsible.

Clearly there's a line between autonomy within a group and anarchy. Equally plainly, we didn't quite get it right. Perhaps we should have established limits. If we did, they ignored them. We should definitely have put a more powerful and knowledgeable financial person in the business. Control from London, a thousand miles away, did not stop independent action, as we saw. One of our own people, I'd say now, would have been best. (Mighty ITT had a financial person in every company they owned, reporting not to the president of the local company, but direct to the financial director in New York. Perhaps I see why now.)

What would you add to my analysis? What would you have done?

Curiously, that bad set-back didn't stop us working in Sweden. Our biggest projects came later.

Kockums

If you take the ferry from Copenhagen to Malmö in Sweden, across the Sound, you pass the giant crane that towers over what was Kockums, a bustling shipyard. For a time that yard was like almost no other in the world. It could put a 350,000 ton supertanker in the water in forty days. Only the Japanese were any competition. One reason for its success was the company's labour relations. They were exemplary. The company's head of communications, Klas Helsing, an exceptionally intuitive and effective man, had a film made to explain the company to the workforce. The film was frank and open and let people have their say – 'I wouldn't let a son of mine work in a place like this,' said one worker; 'hear the noise.' The film was shown widely and won top film awards in the United States. I was so impressed I undertook to show it in Britain, then torn daily by strikes. I managed to get union bosses to one showing. We ran the film in our offices. When it was over I asked the union men what they thought. One was laughing. 'It's like that moral re-armament rubbish,' he said dismissively. Another, a Scot, said, 'Where's the conflict?' I replied, 'There isn't any, that's the point of the film.' 'There's got to be conflict,' spat the Scot.

We'd met Kockums through a friend in London who handled their PR in Britain. Klas Helsing invited us to design a new corporate identity for the yard. We studied the company thoroughly. While building supertankers was their obvious strength, they had others. One company in the group made forestry equipment – lumbering, screeching vehicles that could cut, strip and stack a tree in hardly more than a minute. Terribly, they tore through a forest, razing it before your eyes. Another company made industrial equipment, and there were more. Our recommendations suggested that perhaps their position was not as balanced as it might be. Too many eggs were in the same basket. Prophetically, we showed a slide forecasting the growth in demand for oil tankers of all sizes. Strong as their presence in the shipbuilding industry was, we saw dangers in their dependence on it. We thought they should bring forward their other, impressive interests. Their strategy and hence their corporate identity, we argued, should be that of a balanced, diversified group, not solely a shipyard. Further, they intended to build two LNG (liquid nitrogen gas) carriers. We proved the market wasn't large enough and begged them not to. They paid no attention to that, but they did commission the design phase of our work. In turn they approved this and with the help of Klas Helsing we implemented the programmes thoroughly.

Then what happened? The 1974 oil crisis, when the Arab states quadrupled the price of oil overnight. Suddenly no one wanted supertankers, nor LNGs. Orders dried up. We met Helsing often to think what to do. Finally, an inspiration: we arranged for the president of Kockums, Per Hallenborg, to meet an advisor, Sir Peter Tennant, an old friend of ours. He knew Sweden well. Before the war he'd studied Scandinavian languages, then taught them at Cambridge. He spent the war 'cloak and daggering' in Sweden. He served in the embassy in Paris when Duff Cooper was ambassador, was the first British 'deputy' in Berlin, had been director of the British National Export Council and travelled all over the world. He knew everywhere, everyone and everything – although the latter not deeply. That was the point of bringing them together. Sir Peter has what may be called a 'horizontal' mind: he is aware of a vast range of things and is able to make links between them. Hallenborg, by contrast, has, in this context, a 'vertical' mind. No one in the world knew more about making supertankers than he did; he knew about every computer program, every weld, every rivet. But what do you do when no one wants that knowledge?

Hallenborg, perhaps with reluctance, agreed to see Tennant. They met in a small, plain room immediately after lunch. After a brief preamble, Hallenborg acknowledged that, due to the oil crisis, the yard was short of orders. 'Just out there', said Sir Peter, waving in the direction of the North Sea, 'is the oil business. I happen to know that BP wants two cable-laying ships now. Why not go after those?' No, said Hallenborg, we make supertankers. 'Well,' said Sir Peter, 'Nigeria is just coming on-stream. Why don't you get in touch with – [the Nigerian minister of trade]? He's a charming man. See if you can supply tankers to move his oil.' No, said Hallenborg, who didn't like foreigners (especially black ones, as he'd gaffed on television). The conversation wore on. One of Kockums' interests was in a chemical pad that changed colour with temperature. It was used to check that frozen food had stayed cold. 'There's a marvellous man at Harvard,' said Tennant, 'who's doing interesting work in that field. Maybe someone could go to see him.' There was no answer. After an hour Hallenborg stood up. The meeting was over. As he left the room he said, 'We will get another order this year.' They never did. The Government, against its will, forcibly merged Kockums with another Swedish yard, making it one of Sweden's very few nationalized industries.

Helsing generously wrote later, 'If only we'd taken your advice . . . Your material was, indeed, far-sighted . . . we were, as you indicated, quickly moving from well-known situations to new products, new markets, new people. As it turned out, we did not move quickly enough.'

Ability to adapt

Apart from showing, once more, that design is deeper than what you see on the surface, or at least it should be, the moral of this story, for me, is the value of the 'horizontal' mind in times of change. When conditions are constant, detailed knowledge of one's subject may be a determinant of success, as Kockums showed. When times change that same focus can drag you down. Then the ability to adapt, to see things freshly, make new links, is more useful. That speaks well for a broad, classical education, and for creative thinking.

Someone once said, 'There's no such thing as good writing, only good rewriting.' So it is with selling. It can take years to make a sale. The great thing is to persevere, to keep at it unrelentingly. 'No,' as someone else has said, is a basis for negotiation. Once you have a prospect in mind, you have to keep thinking what his or her changing needs might be, or what new ammunition you've got that might convince him or her now. You have to see the prospect keeps you in mind. 'In sight, in mind' is a good maxim. 'If at first you don't succeed, give up and try something else' may be good for debutant golfers, but is bad for business.

It took us seven or eight years to break into LM Ericsson. They dominate the telephone, electric and electronic industry in Sweden. They have offices in sixty-five countries and are always a serious competitor for national telephone systems. But you'd never have guessed it to look at them.

Our Swedish office had designed products for them, which gave me an opening to talk about their corporate identity. Both with and without Sigvard Bernadotte I had tried repeatedly. The head of corporate affairs, G. O. Douglas, had been with Aga, and I'd tried to sell to him there. Because he'd seen corporate identity work in his old firm, he knew its value and understood what we wanted to do for LM Ericsson. He arranged several meetings with the president of the company, Mr Lundvall, but try as we might, we never had the faintest success.

One day I received a call from Stockholm. It was G. O. Tragically, he said, Mr Lundvall had just been killed – by an elk. Would we go over? Peter Cree and I went. That meeting, a flowering from a seed planted years ago and nurtured since, led to a world-wide programme of work which has lasted years. Peter Cree led the project with Werner Strauli, a gentle, gentlemanly, extremely experienced Swiss designer in the company. One looked after the analytical and management side, the other led all creative meetings and work. They were two experienced people with complementary skills. G. O. later wrote to them: 'Thanks to the speed and efficiency of your company . . . the world-wide programme is now completely accepted and has been implemented . . . you deserve a lot of praise.'

The benefit was not simply a better appearance for the firm, one good design replacing umpteen bad ones. It changed the way Ericsson behaved.

Ericsson's was an exemplary programme. By now we were good at getting and running international business.

5 Heart of the Common Market: Brussels

In the loo of the Garrick I met Ian Harvey, an MP and director of
Yardley, a client of ours. I told him, rather proudly, that we were
planning to open an office in Brussels. 'You're mad,' he said,
'Amsterdam's the place.' It was my turn to think him mad. Amster-
dam? They speak Dutch there. I may have known more about
Amsterdam than Albania, but not much.

Brussels it was to be. For years I'd been prophesying that for
Britain to join the Common Market was 'the great inevitability of our
time'. Believing that Brussels would be the capital or centre of it, and
that all business would flock there, we should be there too. Was it not
our strategy to become the leading design group in Europe? Wasn't
Brussels ideally placed, a few miles by good roads from all the main
cities of Europe? Did they not speak French, a language we could
cope with? For those reasons, to install ourselves in Brussels was the
linchpin of our strategy. We had thought it out; we had researched it.

Too bad our reasoning was wrong!

Parts of the country are lovely; the Grand Place in Brussels, where I
once watched knights in armour jousting before the king, is one of
the wonders of Europe; the romance of the Duchess of Richmond's
ball on the eve of Waterloo where, as Byron wrote, 'the lamps shone
o'er fair women and brave men'; Waterloo itself, unchanged,
Uxbridge's leg still there. There is much in Belgium to cherish.

Entranced by the history, excited at the prospect of this first step
into the heartland of Europe, I went to Brussels several times to learn
what I could. I braved the embassy. They couldn't have been more
welcoming, knowledgeable or helpful. John Wraight (now Sir John),
the commercial counsellor, was the most exceptionally able man.
John Doorbar, his assistant, was wonderful too. We were sure we
couldn't succeed without local knowledge. We intended to acquire a
small, good quality design firm. The British Embassy put us on to
various people. One was Mme Josine des Cressonnières, a strikingly
beautiful widow who ran the Belgian Design Centre with style,
persuasiveness and a will of iron.

Hers was not an easy job. Nor, apart from a few choice pieces, had she much Belgian work to show. It seemed to me that by being in Belgium, doing our best to promote design and get it accepted in industry, we could be useful to her, an ally. Courteously but icily, she said she didn't see it that way. The Belgian government funded her to help Belgian designers, not us. We were invaders pillaging the market. We never really managed to thaw that ice.

It is a point: it must be sensible to strive to be accepted locally. US consultancy firms come to England once in a while; some don't make much effort to serve the local community and I think they're poorer for it.

Being a small band, designers in Brussels soon heard we were coming. One day in London I took a phone call from a stranger. He'd been in partnership in Belgium with a highly regarded designer. He'd heard we were opening an office. Could he come to talk about it? His enterprise, that ear to the ground, that 'get up and go', together with his design experience, were just what we needed. We were impressed.

Quietly, I went to Brussels to check him out. Yes, his partner was a very good designer. Yes, the office was well-regarded. Josine des Cressonnières raised the only jarring note: '*Il est méfiant, cet homme*,' she said. Although I knew it meant she didn't trust him, my French wasn't good enough to appreciate the force of the word. I remember taking in her criticism and being warned by it, but I also observed that she liked his partner very much. Perhaps she was unconsciously biased, I thought. There's a danger that when your heart is set on something you hear what you want to hear. In another language that risk doubles.

We went ahead. We bought the rump of the design practice and changed its name to ours. The enterprising man became head of the business in Belgium. He found offices, hired staff, started working.

Government help

It was in Brussels that I first saw how marvellous British government services for business can be.

In Brussels, Bonn, the Hague, Oslo, Stockholm, Singapore, Tokyo, Washington, New York, Boston, and I'm sure elsewhere, people in the British embassies and consulates have given detailed advice, made introductions, arranged talks, opened doors we could never have opened. It always amazes me how few British people, keen to do business abroad, ever bother to talk to them. Perhaps they do but are disappointed by the response. If you ask general questions, you'll get general answers. I started that way, then realized they weren't much help. Ask specific questions and you'll get specific answers. It is another sign of the need to focus your thinking.

For our tiny Brussels office of five or six people, the embassy helped us majestically. They arranged a party for us at the Amigo Hotel, then the best in Brussels. Over 100 senior business executives attended. The ambassador, Sir Roderick Barclay, spoke and we made a brief presentation as well as having a static display, mostly brought from London.

How, I asked Sir John Wraight later, had they attracted over 100 people? That morning, he told me, his office had telephoned everyone invited to confirm that he or she would come. It was an object lesson: such thoroughness is almost essential to succeed internationally.

ITT

Seeing Brussels as the natural home for us because it was the centre of the Common Market was logic that hardly worked. Although there were exceptions (ICI was one company in Brussels we worked for), almost all of our work in Belgium was for Belgian companies. Most international firms had not set up in Brussels. Those that had did their design at home. Nor, we discovered, is Brussels the take-off point for other European cities. In our world designers coming from London proved far more acceptable than any from Belgium.

None the less, ITT made up for everything. One day the boss of our Belgian office phoned. He'd heard ITT were coming to town. If he could fix it, would I come over to meet them? 'Who,' I asked 'are ITT?' 'Just one of the biggest firms in the world,' he replied. I went.

ITT's Consumer Products Group, whom we met, started modestly. They had just moved into new, carpeted, offices. Desks and lights and filing cabinets were being moved in. The vice-president, Jim Goodson, invited us to visit, at our expense, three television manufacturing companies they'd bought, in Britain, France and Germany. We were to see whether we could be useful to them. He was giving us the chance to demonstrate our value to ITT. His idea worked beautifully. When we returned some weeks later we were able to talk to ITT executives in real terms that applied to them. That is so much better than talk of how clever we'd been with other firms.

Twenty years ago TV sets in each country were made independently and without any relationship to any other manufacturer. A chassis produced in France, say, would be a centimetre or two larger or smaller than the one made in Britain, different again from the one made in Germany. There was ample room for rationalization, so the components could be made in larger volume and shipped around. The designs of all sets were commonplace. They offered the same performance and were sold for the same price everywhere. Or to be more exact, competitors cut prices to sell. That, we argued, was no way to do business. It was vital to 'break out of the price prison', as we put it.

Brainstorm in Brussels

In London we'd held a series of 'brainstorming' sessions to imagine how this might be done. The presentation we gave ITT was so creative that its benefit lasted for years. Why, we asked, did all TV sets have to be the same size? (This was before the small and large sets you can buy today.) We showed sketches of small sets a decade before the first came from Japan. Why, we wondered, did all TV sets have to offer the same performance? Couldn't some be built to provide better quality than normal? Couldn't we offer a set that offered less but cost less? Schaub-Lorenz in Germany explored this and found that they could take 30 per cent off the cost of a set. Why should all TV sets be the same, regardless of what sort of customer wanted to buy? We showed sketches of TV sets as fashion items, with movable panels to alter the colour scheme, others for children, another for the kitchen. There was much more.

ITT gave us a day to present our ideas. They were pleased. Jim Goodson thought we could help his companies, growing in number by the day, but as each was profit-responsible, Jim felt unwilling to impose us on them. He would make the introduction; we'd have to make our own case. That worked too. Over the next few years we designed refrigerators for their appliance company in Norway, radios in Germany, household products in the Netherlands, washing-machines in Belgium, food packaging in Germany, cosmetics packaging in France . . . eight countries in all.

Those were high days in ITT. Every month Harold Geneen would arrive from New York in his own Boeing, together with a large team of number-crunchers. The company, hard and numerate, gave us the best education we could have had. In time we came to know executives throughout Europe and, earning every job on our merits, were well-installed as their designers. Better, we got to know Jim Goodson. As clear-eyed and numerate as any manager, he had the foresight to see the value of design, and possessed powers of imagination quite exceptional in business.

Jim Goodson

An American with slicked-down hair, dark eyes and a pencil-thin moustache, Jim Goodson dressed elegantly. Outdoors he wore a light coat with velvet collar and often sported a grey bowler hat tilted rakishly on his head. In Jermyn Street that might have been unremarkable; in Brussels it revealed his personality. He is a fine man. In Paris when the war started, he made his way to England to go home. He sailed in the Athenia, the first liner to be sunk in the war. Rescuing drowning people, he distinguished himself. Then, back in Liverpool, he joined the Royal Air Force. He became a Spitfire pilot, one of only seven Americans to fight in the Battle of Britain. He flew with the Eagle Squadron (his name is on the winged statue in Grosvenor Square).

Stationed in Kent, flying into mortal combat five or six times a day from bombed airfields, he and other officers were befriended by a local lord. They'd sleep better in his house, he said, and offered them a wing of it for their own use. At all hours of the day and night pilots, often well-watered, would roar up to the great gates in their MGs and the gateman who lived in the lodge would let them in. At Christmas the pilots wanted to give him a present. Jim, deputed to do this, offered him cash. 'Oh, no,' said the gateman, he couldn't take their money. 'His lordship pays me,' he explained. 'But,' protested Jim, 'I'm sure a little more would help. I mean, what does his lordship pay you?' 'Well, nothing actually,' said the gateman, 'but it is regular.'

Jim moved to the US Air Force when America entered the war. He had the rare distinction of wearing RAF wings over one breast and US wings over the other. He transferred to Mustangs, escorting Flying Fortresses on their long-range daylight bombing raids. He shot down thirty-five German aircraft, then was shot down himself when he destroyed the first German jet fighter on the ground at Templehof airfield in Berlin.

Working for ITT cast a long and good shadow.

A marketing man from ITT came to see us in London one day. He was wearing one of the first calculator watches. By each figure on the dial was a button – a good idea. If I say 586, you know at once where the buttons are. On the face of the watch was a screen. Touch another button and you could see the time in up to three time zones. Rudely I remarked, 'What a shame that with all the technology all you can do is add up and tell the time in places you don't want to go.'

That's one way ideas come. A few days later Roger Ford, who'd headed our product design team and was now in charge of product development at Milton Bradley, the American toy firm, came in. 'You remember the game Battleships we all played as children?' he said. 'I wonder if we can't turn that into a modern game.' Someone thought of the watch we'd seen. What would happen, we wondered, if you put a microchip into a game? The result was Computer Battleships, the first electronic game. In three years its sales exceeded £25 million. From that start Milton Bradley launched one highly successful electronic game after another.

Within a week or two of the quadrupling of oil prices in 1974, Jim Goodson came to the office. By now he was boss of a several-billion-dollar business in Europe. He sat down and looked at us and said in his quiet, gentle voice, 'I guess you wonder why I'm here.' Yes. 'The world we know has come to an end. We face new situations. We need people who are experienced in new situations or in adapting existing resources to suit new situations.' Then, after a pause, he added, 'I guess that's you.'

I took that not only as a compliment and testament to all the work we'd done for his companies, but also as a definition of what designers ought to be.

Exhibition in Moscow

The Brussels office grew. We designed products, packaging, and corporate identities. Then, curiously, we found the office doing more and more exhibition design, for which we had little taste in London. The Belgian designers were designing exhibition stands all over Europe, from Milan (for Ideal Standard) to Moscow (for the Belgian government). So successful were they that we brought the Belgians to Britain to design stands for British firms who wanted to show abroad.

Revenue in Brussels mounted nicely – one million francs, two million – but there was never any profit. We couldn't understand it. Slow-witted and trusting, it took me months to realize that every time I met the head of the office he wore a better watch, drove a bigger BMW, had more fur on his coat collar. And he moved into a new house. A good man in the office, Pierre Van Win, warned me but wouldn't be specific.

The boss was twisting us. I raised it at the board in London. What evidence was there? None, just a feeling. Douglas Scott, my colleague, said, 'We've employed this man to run the company; we should trust him.' Weakly, I acquiesced. We should have been more rigorous. I have to say with sadness that all those nice English ideas of fairness and trust didn't fit here.

In the end we worked out what the Belgian was doing. An excellent salesman, the Belgian was winning lots of exhibition work. His office, our office, would do the design. All the construction, shipping, erection and demounting was given to one firm of contractors who padded their contracts and our man took a good cut. Between them they shared the profit. In the end, we hired an expensive firm of accountants to go through all the books for the previous two years. They calculated the extent of the robbery. We confronted the boss and asked him to pay it back. If he didn't, we said, we would go back another two years. He agreed at once. The court signed an order against him. He paid three instalments then disappeared.

Opening an office in another country is never easy. Sadly, normal goodwill and trust isn't always enough. Distant offices provide rich opportunities for the greedy. It may be unfair, but today I'd always put my own experienced, trusted man or woman in charge of a foreign office. You need someone who knows the firm's ways, who is loyal to the firm and whose future lies with it. We tried with varying degrees of success to insist our own financial systems were used. Several of us wrestled with budgets and balances in half the accounting systems of Europe. Even if the intention was not to fool us, poor accounting methods led to incomprehension which helped no one.

After several years, the Belgian office ran aground. We could have saved it. I thought of going there for six months, which would have done it. But I didn't.

Design and marketing

One discouragement was that we were never accepted by the Belgian design community. Because Josine des Cressonnières was friendly with the director of the Design Council in London, Paul Reilly (now Lord Reilly), her low opinion of us also spread back to England. That was hardly fair, although it was true that they shared a cultural view of design different from ours.

Whenever we met businessmen or journalists we argued that 'design is a function of marketing'. It was our job, therefore, to help companies create products people want to buy, and to help them compete in other ways. To Josine des Cressonnières that was vulgar pandying to the masses.

The embassy arranged for me to give quite an important talk in Brussels. There was a large audience. I'd written the talk in my poor French, to keep it colloquial and to use words I could say, then had had it turned into good French. My apparent fluency misled the audience into thinking I speak better French than I do. Questions came at high speed. One, from the chairman of the Design Centre, was about design and marketing. It was forceful but also complex and rambling. After a while his voice lifted. He'd asked a question, it seemed. I looked blank, then said, 'Oui.' The audience roared with laughter, at what I had no idea.

If the design fraternity didn't understand our view of marketing, clients did. Philippe Rasquinet, a product designer whose father had owned the copper works in Liège, joined us in London even though he could not speak a word of English. His wife used to coach him over the kitchen table at night. As he improved, Philippe became responsible for our work in Belgium. Each week he'd take his car to Belgium and roar along the autoroutes at immense speed, seeking clients. Thanks to his persistence and patience we won long design programmes from some of the largest companies in the country. FN, the arms dealer diversifying into sports goods, was one. Innovation Bon-Marché, the supermarket and retailing group, was another, Nagelmackers, a small private bank, a third.

By now our service was superb. All meetings were in French, all documentation and design was flawlessly correct. We worked at various levels in each company, so maintained good relations for a long time.

Perhaps because we were not fully accepted by the official establishment, we never got into Sabena. We tried hard enough. We'd often crossed the Channel in Sabena aircraft, but had no experience of their bigger fleet. To experience it at first hand, I flew from New York to Brussels, all in a spirit of fact-finding. It was dreadful: thin, mean seats, sparse service, all uncaring. Our knowledge of corporate identity and internal communications, combined with research we'd done into the aviation industry and our direct experience, meant we had plenty to say. But we were never given a serious chance to say it. Sabena always refused our requests to visit them.

Belgian Steel

For years Philippe Rasquinet tried to sell into Cockerill, essentially the Belgian steel industry. He'd built very good links at lower and mid-levels in the group, but no one was able to interest the president. Philippe asked me to help. Sir John Wraight was now on our board as a non-executive director. Together we went to see the embassy people in Brussels, who offered to brief us. Over lunch at Le Cygne, we talked about the company, the plight of the steel industry in Belgium and about the president himself, M. Charlier. He'd come from IBM. He has a chip on his shoulder about graduates – if you've got five Nobel prize-winners on your staff, we were advised, for heaven's sake don't say so. He's a fanatic about punctuality. Your only hope, they said, is to go for a meeting first thing in the morning!

The meeting was set for 8 a.m. in Liège. Setting off while it was still pitch black, we drove from Brussels. At 7.50 a.m. we reached Charlier's office. At eight o'clock precisely a man came towards us. Impassively, with scarcely a '*bonjour*', he showed us to a room, then waved us to sit at a round table. He sat too. This was Charlier. We waited for him to speak. He waited for us. After a long moment I launched into our prepared story. Carefully scripted to conserve his time, it was succinct. During the monologue (it was hardly a conversation), I mentioned a man in the office who had a Ph.D. in physics. Sir John glared at me. At 8.30, on the dot, Charlier stood. The meeting was over. He said we should talk to someone he named, shook hands and went. That, a culmination of considerable effort, was that.

Hours later an elated manager told Philippe Rasquinet we had got the job. Without a sign, the president had appointed us to undertake an extremely thorough study. The steel industry was full of problems. Cockerill was losing money heavily, and facing fierce union opposition. M. Charlier appreciated, evidently, that clearer communications could help. Over the next couple of years we worked intimately with the company, developing new strategies for their communications and new designs.

That was such a model sale it is worth analysing. Philippe Rasquinet came from Liège. He knew the company and was accepted as a local by people in it. Equally in our favour, they might have thought that a local design company would not have known enough to solve their problems. Perhaps because M. Charlier had experience in the United States and of using consultancies, it was accepted that as a London company of some scale and experience by then, we would have the advanced knowledge and competence they needed.

As well as the knowledge of Cockerill Philippe had garnered over years in the company, we used our information department in London to learn more. We knew a lot about both Cockerill and the steel industry in general. That came through. We sought advice from the embassy, and it was as precise as telling us what time of day was best to try to get an appointment with M. Charlier, and something of his attitudes and prejudices. I fancy the embassy actually made the appointment for us. As well as meeting the president, Philippe and I had met (and Philippe knew well) people at several layers of the company. In other words we were selling *in depth*, something we believed in. We could hope that if the president asked his colleagues, they would support our proposals.

We were punctual. We tailored our brief presentation as precisely as we knew how to the man we were talking to. We spoke in French. We had prepared answers to every question he might raise. We assumed the president wouldn't doubt our ability to design well. Names of firms we'd worked for would reassure him of that. Instead, we focused on the difficult problems, which he knew so well, of implementation, of effecting change in a large organization. That was precisely right.

The work programme, too, was a model. Every stage was budgeted and agreed. Philippe, in charge of the project and there most weeks, insisted on providing exemplary service.

When the time came to present our design, again we did so to layers of management, listening to their views, carrying them with us. When we saw the president, we briefly showed that lots of work had been done, letting him flip through dozens of rough sketches. Then we focused on two different schemes. Each would have done. One was, in our view, more advanced than the other. Charlier found himself choosing between the two. He decided on the more advanced design.

Flemish fanatic

Even though we worked through Cockerill from top to toe, we never visited their plants in Flemish Belgium. You could have cut the antagonism between the two parts of the country with a pair of scissors.

We have seen that before. While we still had the office in Brussels our local boss rang. He'd got into Agfa-Gevaert. They were in Antwerp. Would I go with him? 'Be careful,' I was advised. 'They're the most Flemish company in Belgium. Speak English.' We were well-received, offered coffee and small cigars. Speaking in English, we got on well. After a while our host turned to my colleague and asked a question in French. My friend replied in French. Immediately, as if stung by a bee, the Agfa man turned to me and said, sharply, 'When you are in our country speak our language. Come back when you've learnt that.' He all but threw us out. He'd set a trap and we'd fallen in it.

Where's the moral in that? We'd been advised . . . Unless times have changed, it shows what a difficult country Belgium is to work in, or rather that it is smaller and more parochial than you'd think. None the less, even after our office in Brussels closed, we did a great deal of work there. That is entirely due to the doggedness of Philippe Rasquinet. Week after week he'd drive through drizzle and the greyness of dawn to visit one company after another. His homework was always excellent, his service as good. His success is evidence of the importance of 'stickability' in international business. Perhaps this means that you don't actually need an office in the country, though you *do* need nationals of the country. I'm sure that made a difference.

6 Year In, Year Out: The Netherlands

Dutchmen can be fun; I'd seen that. When the Olympic Games were held in London in 1948 a number of Dutch students worked at the fancifully styled Olympic Village – actually the RAF station at Uxbridge. Some British students worked there too, me among them. One man, from Oxford, had the conceit of wearing his blazer with the collar turned up. One day the Dutch students held a party to honour Fanny Blankerskoen, who had won four gold medals. They all arrived in pyjama jackets (the nearest they could get to striped blazers), with the collar turned up.

Dutch students turned their collars up

Years later when my firm was new, I was in Padua with the European Packaging Federation. (At that time, typically, the English were not members but 'observers'.) At a café called the Leon Bianco we ate outside at a long table under an awning. A senior executive from Unilever, a Dutchman, hired a crippled guitarist to play and sing for us. He perched on the table itself and his music drew a flock of onlookers. The Dutchman picked up a plate and went among them, collecting money. He got enough to pay for the same guitarist for the next two evenings. On one of those evenings it rained so we ate indoors. The same Dutchman appeared from the kitchen on a bicycle, holding a plate of food above his head. That slight experience, amplified since, makes it impossible not to hold Dutch people in the highest esteem. We came to love them.

Even so, the idea of selling there was beyond me. As history shows, that was terribly ignorant. The Netherlands, without question, was the most fulfilling and most enjoyable country we ever worked in – and other British firms would say the same.

Perhaps it is salutary to note that we went to Amsterdam by chance. Much as we believed in planning, the Netherlands wasn't part of our scheme. I'd given a talk at the Management Centre Europe, in Brussels. At the end a man offered me his card and suggested I visit him. He came from a firm I'd never heard of, Albert Heijn, a supermarket group. Before meeting the man, I went to a number of their shops. They were not impressive. Some were small, no more than corner stores. Others were larger, very cheap and aggressive to my eye. Windows were plastered with one slashed-price offer after another, vile posters of an ugly man pointing his thumb down.

Albert Heijn was run by two delightful brothers who were admired throughout the Netherlands. The company's image didn't reflect them at all. The man I met was the design manager, Mr Jonkher. Quiet and diffident, he was firm and capable none the less. His own taste was exquisite. He had it in mind to ask us to develop a new identity for the company and for the stores.

Homework works

We got the job; John Harris was the designer. His presentation to the brothers, Mr Jonkher and others, was an object lesson. John had created a design that was light blue and white, using an abstract symbol concocted from the initials AH. His work was uncompromisingly modern. Albert Heijn's advertising agent was present. When the presentation was over and opinions were sought, the advertising man attacked John's typography. He called it poor, indeed, amateur. My heart sank. This, after all, was our first job in Holland.

John Harris had used a new letter style, created by a Professor Hollenstein in Paris. He had, it is true, taken liberties with it, condensing some letters, extending others, to add visual interest to the Albert Heijn name. How was he to respond to the outburst? Without a word he drew from his briefcase a letter and handed it to the advertising man. The letter was from Professor Hollenstein. It thanked John for letting him see the proposed use of his lettering, and congratulated him. He thought it good.

Round one to John, but there was more to come. John recommended a light but vibrant blue for the trucks, of which there were several hundred. The transport manager, in the room, objected to the colour. 'There's no such colour available,' he said. 'One like this will fade in no time,' he added. That sounded a more serious criticism. One of the Heijn brothers looked at John quizzically. So, in a more anguished way, did I. How little faith! John pulled from his briefcase a sheaf of letters. They were from the three firms that supplied paint for the vehicles. Each agreed they could match the colour sample John had sent. They confirmed, too, that it fell within Albert Heijn's exacting performance standards.

I never saw more compelling proof of the power of good research. Homework works. We were lucky to learn that so early in our business lives. John's design was accepted not simply for its style or appropriateness, but because he had found out first that it worked in every detail. Not all design, it must be said, is so thorough. Designers often put forward concepts that don't work or can't be made. To do so is as foolish and damaging as it is lazy.

An Amsterdam office

The programme for Albert Heijn worked wonderfully. Within a few months we were doing so much for them that they thought we should open a local office. The logic runs like this. There are two phases of a design project. The first needs the most experience and best thought you can find. Time and money matter less than the quality of work. Whether the design office is in Milan or Montevideo doesn't matter much. But once the concept is presented and approved, then the rules change. Time and money become paramount. Speed and economy of implementation become the new yardsticks. That is why Albert Heijn wanted us to be near them.

We were all for it. Albert Heijn introduced us to a designer they used a lot, a Dutchman, with his own local office. We got on well. He agreed we should work together; indeed, we would buy the majority of stock in his company. But Peter Cree forecast a serious shortage of business in the coming year. These were the days of Labour government, when one downturn followed another (if you could run a company in Britain in those days you could run one anywhere). He feared that if we diverted our Dutch work into a new office we would suffer in London. Peter remember, was a navigator – always cautious, always sure, always safe.

What should we do? Buy the Dutch company and build our work with Albert Heijn but risk losing money – and even jobs – at home? Or play safe? Perhaps because we had gone so far in our talks and wanted to keep Albert Heijn, I said carry on. But Peter prevailed. I took his advice. We did not establish that office in the Netherlands. Our work with Albert Heijn did dwindle, but we stayed in business in London profitably. Peter was probably right. What would you have done?

A survey in *Time* magazine once showed that entrepreneurs are not the swashbucklers of popular imagination; they can be quite conservative. Or maybe that is just the successful ones.

When to cut?

Even harder than knowing when to start something is knowing when to stop it. I've cut some activities too soon, and let others drag on too long. With hindsight, I'd say the latter is more damaging. When something goes wrong you pour more and more effort into turning it round. The risk is that you focus on failure. We do better to concentrate on and reinforce the successful parts of our companies.

We saw Beecham cut a whole new range of DIY products we'd created for them. They had been greeted with enthusiasm. Early tests were more than encouraging. Then, tragically, the project manager in Beecham, the man who had steered the programme so well, was murdered. (I was interviewed in the office by a barrel-chested man who styled himself 'Diamond of the Yard'.) The chief executive stopped the project we'd worked on. Years later I showed it to men who'd risen to the board. 'That decision to stop', one said, 'cost us millions.'

Timing is so difficult. The Netherlands was one prime case of getting the timing right. Eric Baskerville, a tall, rangy, cadaverous-looking man who smoked Gaulois incessantly, joined us from Lintas, then the Unilever advertising agency. We hired him to get and manage business in Holland. For six months nothing happened. I was worried, but wiser people persuaded me to continue with him. After another six months still not much had happened. Again, others in the firm urged me to have faith. Thank heaven for them. In one burst Eric came good and stayed good for years. More than any one man, he built our business in the Netherlands. Thanks to him we did far more work in the Netherlands than any other design office, including Dutch ones.

In time many designers came to have plenty of experience of flying back and forth. We had more than one Dutchman working as a client service manager, a Dutch secretary, as well as the British back-up staff. We all got on well, but it was Eric the clients wanted to see. They loved him, as we all did. 'The nicest Englishman in Holland,' they called him. So good was his service, many believed he lived there.

Having worked for Albert Heijn helped a lot. It is so well-regarded that other companies in the Netherlands accepted our credentials readily. Eric got us into Shell, then Akzo, which had grown by merging a chemical business with one selling salt. We visited salt mines. Eric got and serviced a long-running design programme with what is now ABN Bank (we changed the name from Algemene Bank Nederland on the grounds that while everyone in Holland could say that, no one else could, and their future was bound to be more international).

Into Philips

Philips was another company we worked for. Knut Yran, a Norwegian (we were confident his name was made up), was in charge of design there. His successor, Bob Blaich, couldn't be more different. Bob, an American from Herman Miller in Zeeland, Michigan, the distinguished furniture firm, is a systems person; Yran was talk and style and expense account. But to him goes the credit for getting the board of what was a monolithic, staid company to think about design. Not easy in a vast technical company like that. He persuaded Philips to do something about its identity around the world (everywhere, that is, except the United States, where Philips works under the name Norelco). It was a mess. There was no consistency. Yran appointed us to put order in it. It was a substantial job, covering every letterhead, every invoice, every package, vehicle, product, even aircraft.

Wonderful. But there was a catch. Every item we designed had to be approved by Philips' legal department. There were 150 lawyers in Eindhoven alone, all vying to be the most conservative.

And Knut Yran drove us mad. Because he changed or 'corrected' everything, then changed it again, planning, so essential in a project of that scale, became impossible. The job took months longer and devoured more designers and others than we envisaged. He had insisted on a fixed-fee contract, so we lost money as well as patience.

From that we learnt how important it is to be precise about the amount of work you expect to do for the fee that is agreed. If you can't be sure, then the financial arrangement must be based on the fact that neither you nor the client knows. Ever since our experience with Mitchelstown Creameries in Ireland, it had been our practice to charge extra for modifications made by the client to our designs. But Yran wouldn't pay. He would change our work, often capriciously in our view, then expect us to redo everything at our expense. We strengthened our conditions of contract so that this trouble, so far as I know, never arose again.

Notwithstanding the tensions, this, our first global project, went through to the end. Philips had never used outside designers before. When the corporate identity work was complete, Yran brought in our product designers. People in our Stockholm office redesigned the Philips razor.

We should thank Philips for aiding our own development. Knut Yran and the 150 lawyers were fanatical about detail, so we learnt to be too. Another thing: in Yran's office was a poster which read, 'The memory of quality lasts longer than the memory of price.' It took me a while to realize the significance of that. Then I understood: deliver the quality, and the money will look after itself.

Designers work direct

It was always our practice to have designers work directly with clients. Some design offices don't do that. They have 'middle-men' who sell the job, brief the designers, collect their work, then present it to the client. A couple of years ago a design office in New York hired me to look at their business and suggest improvements. In that office, a well-known one, designers never meet clients. The boss doesn't see the need, nor would he allow the expense.

It is a foolish economy. Not knowing the clients, never having visited their offices or plant or seen their products in stores, designers aim in the dark. Worse, they feel little interest in the clients or desire to help them prosper. The go-betweens find it difficult too; they can't always explain a design as well as its creator can. Our view was that designers work much better if they see for themselves the people and firm they are serving. If they immerse themselves in the companies they work for and feel responsible for the quality of work done, their effort and enthusiasm is immensely enhanced.

In the Netherlands this policy surprised some people. But they came to see its strength and enjoyed working face-to-face with designers.

Our practice varied to suit the client and the individual. Some designers managed all aspects of the project. More often, they were teamed with what would now be called a design manager. He or she would look after the work programme and agree each phase with the client. They would see meetings were arranged and everything worked on time, to budget. At working meetings and creative reviews, client service managers would see that the objective was kept clearly in mind, remind people of the brief, and say whatever they wanted to say. But they could not tell the designer what to design or over-rule any design. Because the designers had seen the client company themselves and studied all the competitors and other issues, they were well able to know what to do.

In any design office studio artists are the unsung heroes. They're the ones who work all hours to allow you to meet deadlines. We tried to find reasons for them to visit clients too, or their printers in the Netherlands and elsewhere, so that they would feel as committed to producing excellent work as anyone. The same was true of secretaries, financial people or others. Typing letters to people you've never met about things you don't follow is a heartless life. We tried to involve them in client meetings. You can't imagine the difference that made.

Last day at the Tate

Heribert Sanberg, a young account director from an advertising agency in Amsterdam, came to the office one day. He was looking for designers to create new packaging for a client of theirs, one of the big detergent companies in the Netherlands. His visit was unexpected and irritating, because, untypically, I'd promised myself I'd go to an exhibition at the Tate. We talked for a while then, rather rudely, I said, 'you must forgive me. There's an exhibition at the Tate and today is the last day. I really must go.' As an afterthought, I added, 'You wouldn't care to come, would you?'

He said he would. The exhibition was a decade of modern painting, Rothko, Oldenberg and others. It was amazing: Sanberg not only knew the paintings, he knew most of the painters. Looking at one painting he'd say, 'He's not the same since he took up with that Peruvian girl.' Of another, 'The pot's got him, that's what's wrong with him.' It turned out his father ran the Stedelijk Museum in Amsterdam. He explained modern painting with a vigour and clarity I've never heard equalled. We ate that evening and next day he flew off. Later we heard we'd got the job.

At the Tate, sharing interests

As a sale, that was luck, though I dare say we satisfied the professional side of his visit. If we were to seek a moral, it would be sharing a community of interest with your client, albeit by accident.

We worked for that detergent firm comprehensively for a long time. One day the marketing director told me about a new kind of detergent using enzymes. It was sweeping Holland. I said I was sure he could sell it in England. He demurred; Britain is too big, he hadn't the contacts. I arranged them for him. A British firm took the product. Their test market sales, in the Tyne-Tees area, doubled our client's business. He was happy, but did nothing for us. For a while I was piqued, and tried to think how we could benefit from introductions we made. But that was wrong. The professional consultant has strength if he is seen to be independent, selling nothing but his work. Once, in a city livery company, a supplier of packaging material offered me a percentage if we'd recommend his products. Fortunately, I didn't understand until the moment had passed. I remember thinking much less of the man after that.

Bathrooms and billiard tables

We went to Holland often, staying in all sorts of places and conditions. Late at night, after a long day, Eric Baskerville and I checked into the Hotel Krasnapolsky, off the Dam Square in Amsterdam. A porter showed us to the only available room – a bathroom. We looked at the porter in dismay. With a straight face he assured us that one of us could sleep in the bath and the other on the floor. Eric, the mildest of men, muttered a few Dutch expletives with telling effect. Who'd believe it, there were two bedrooms after all.

In Germany, years later, Jeremy Danks, head of our German operation, wasn't so lucky. He, too, arrived late at the hotel. They, too, were full up. Jeremy waved his letter of confirmation, but there

Offered this bedroom for two in Amsterdam

was nothing for it. No doubt exercising his German, he got the night porter to make up a bed for him on the only available surface, a billiard table. Next morning Jeremy in his silk polka-dot dressing-gown strode through the hotel lobby to the bathroom, head high, past a line of bemused guests waiting to check out.

Not all the travel was like that. For a while my friend Peter Berger (now Vice-Admiral Sir Peter) was naval and military attaché in the Hague. Going to stay with him and his wife June, I dutifully took two bottles of duty-free whisky, as a gift. Peter smiled. He took me to a room and opened the double doors to a large cupboard. There were perhaps 200 bottles of whisky in it. Entertaining was part of their job. In the bathroom instead of a bottle of Alka-Seltzer, there was a case of it. They'd suffer two and sometimes three parties a night. But all diplomats there, he told me, shared a common rule. They were always in bed by midnight.

Dutch tattoo

Peter Berger had to organize a tattoo in Amsterdam. In Dutch that is a '*taptoe*', so in the office we spoke of 'taptoeing through the tulips'. Pat Tilley, a brilliant graphic artist, whose posters 'Top people take *The Times*' have become collector's items, was a colleague at the time. He kindly designed some posters for the tattoo. We gave them to Peter. To thank us, he invited me to the event. As with everything he touched, it was a complete success. He'd drawn British troops from Germany and the UK and they shared the performance with Dutch units. At a certain moment, the lights dimmed. Great doors at the end of the arena swung open. In marched another band; there'd been several already, but this one was different. The band wore the red berets of the Parachute Regiment, a regiment immortal in Dutch eyes because of the Battle of Arnhem. When they marched on, everyone in the packed arena stood up. It was a moving moment and profound comment on the people of the Netherlands.

Earlier, I'd seen the true professionalism of diplomats at work. I was one of dozens or hundreds in a queue to meet the ambassador, Sir Peter Garran, and his wife. As we were introduced, Lady Garran said, 'Oh, Mr Pilditch, I must tell you how much we like your posters.' How she remembered from that mass of people, heaven knows.

We found the same in Washington years later. My wife and I had been invited to a party held on the Queen's birthday in the garden of

the British embassy. We flew down from Boston for it, where we'd
been staying with the son of a painter. As we lined up to meet the
ambassador we saw a painting of the embassy just done by our
friend's father. My wife remarked on this. 'Oh, Tom's here,' said the
ambassador (Sir Peter Ramsbottom). 'He's over there, by that tree,
wearing yellow trousers and a blue coat.' There were two thousand
people on that lawn.

Sir John Wraight was a junior official in Cairo when the British
Embassy was attacked by a mob. With the ambassador, he escaped
the back way. As they climbed a wall and ran across the neighbouring
garden, the ambassador turned to John and said, 'Remind me to send
Mme –' (whose garden it was) 'a bunch of flowers.'

The Beatles

In the 1960s Britain was seen as out-of-date, unprogressive, its
industry poor, its workers lazy. We worked especially hard to overcome that prejudice. The record shows we succeeded, but there's no
doubt the Beatles made a difference. When they hit the world, with
Mary Quant and Carnaby Street before the sleaze, people could see
that young, new ideas were bursting from Britain. Design, too, was
exciting. Designers were imaginative and confident, their creativity
now coupled with professionalism and experience of working for
industry on a large scale.

Part of our promotion effort was to speak at business conferences
wherever we could.

On one occasion I spoke to an Anglo-Dutch group in the Hague on
'Design in Britain'. I expected a small audience. There must have
been five or six hundred people there. I started by playing a tape of
'Penny Lane', the Beatles song, then tried to explain what it meant,
before broadening into the theme of how life, and hence design, was
altering. It was probably not a success. The audience, I was told later,
had been expecting me to talk about Sheraton and Wedgwood.

Travelling so much, I compiled an address book of hotels and
restaurants in dozens of cities. It meant we could arrive in Nijmegen
or s'Hertogenbosch or anywhere and know at once where to stay
modestly and where to eat in a charming restaurant. That book was
invaluable. Then I lost it in Stockholm. For me that's bad because I
have no memory. My wife and I were going to the Far East once, via
Amsterdam. 'We'll eat somewhere nice,' I said, but my mind went
blank. Then a brainwave; Alan Fletcher, at Pentagram, had compiled

a book of recommendations from his friends in design and advertising: where to go in cities around the world. I'd provided a few entries. I found the book and took it to Amsterdam. There, sure enough, was a café I'd recommended highly. We sat through the worst meal, the worst service, in the draftiest room, at the highest price you could imagine.

From his bed on the billard table

When Eric Baskerville retired he left a hole in our hearts as well as in our competence. He had led most of our work in the Netherlands for years. Others from London sustained the business and we recruited more than one client service manager. One was like an infantryman so keen to get into battle that he forgets to take a rifle – for all his vigour, he didn't succeed in Holland because he didn't do his homework. Another, more stable and serious, was Chris Heine, who did well for years. But none of us could match Eric. Is it sentimental to say that really to excel, you need people who touch the hearts of the people they work for and with?

Our experience in the Netherlands was, almost without exception, that companies there are very good. They're organized, decisive, business-like, amiable, friendly, fair. They use creative people well, briefing them carefully, listening to what they say, accepting work that is soundly argued. It may be, too, that Dutch and British attitudes and tastes are not dissimilar. That no doubt helped. We saw in Sweden, for example, how just having a different idea of what is good can make international business much harder.

So there's the irony. We planned to enter Belgium, only to find most of our assumptions wrong. We did not plan to go to Holland, chance took us there, yet we found lots of large companies with sophisticated, forward-looking management, warm, receptive, open, delightful people. Does that mean planning is a waste of time? No. It implies that any plan should have room for flexibility, allowing you to take an opportunity that falls within a broad vision of where you want to go.

The Netherlands did that and helped us develop the skills we had: thoroughness, belief in information, feeling close to our clients, sustained service. Perhaps a new element was the way designers were close to their clients and plainly responsible for doing good work for them. Communications were direct. Loyalty and enthusiasm and commitment, spread throughout the business, was a cardinal reason for success in this market. Being in Holland moved all of us a long way.

7 The Big Game: Germany

As a soldier at the end of the war, a friend of mine was sent to take over, or liberate, the Herman Goering Works in Salzgitter, in Germany. He arrived in a light armoured car, to be met by a crowd of hostile workers. They wouldn't clear a path for him. He called to them to move. Nothing happened. He called again. Still no one budged. The third time he called, 'Stand aside, I am coming forward now.' He tapped the turret to tell his driver to advance. As the scout car drove forward the crowd parted. The vehicle tipped head first into a repair pit.

Time spent in reconnaissance, so runs the army maxim, is seldom wasted.

Germany was always the big one for us. Even after we'd worked on the mainland of Europe for a decade, had fluent and recurring ways of doing business in other countries, we fought shy of Germany. The largest, most efficient, most powerful organized industry in Europe daunted us. The market, we appreciated, was complex, intricate, devolved. None of us knew the country nor was fluent in the language.

Still, the time came to try. The amateurishness of our early approach embarrasses me.

I went to Germany once or twice to see and feel the place. I stayed in Cologne with the same friend. He lived in a penthouse apartment, high above a bend in the Rhine. By then he was busy turning a loss-making subsidiary of a British public company into a profitable jewel in the group's crown.

Back in England I went on a German-language course at the Institute of Directors. It was for three weeks, mornings only. The results, I must say, were remarkable. You learnt phrases, using, you see I remember it now, a *Tonbandgerät*, a tape recorder. I had no idea of the difference between 'dem' and 'den', essential to good grammar, yet a few weeks later I was in the office of an advertising agent in Frankfurt. I asked if I could use his phone. I called a man miles away to say I was sorry I'd miss the train he expected me to be on. I'd take a later train, change somewhere, then take a taxi and be with him by 3.30 p.m. My host said the German was perfect. That is to say, the phrases I'd learnt were grammatically correct.

Designed for businessmen, the course concentrated on terms you'd need to move around, book a room and so forth. Neither then, nor now, have I been able to speak German apart from those few phrases. But if you think how many years we spend at school not learning to speak another language, not daring to try, even that limited ability speaks well for the teaching method.

Where to start?

One of the difficulties of doing business in Germany is to know where to do it. Germany lost Berlin. Imagine the UK without London. Where would you go and in what order? Leeds? Birmingham? Manchester? Liverpool? We chose to concentrate on Frankfurt, though eventually we worked in a good many cities. Why Frankfurt? At the time it seemed to us the most developed city in Germany for our kind of work: you found good advertising agencies, management consultancies, market-research and public-relations consultants there.

From our first forays, our strategy and tactics developed. We focused on our strengths, then gradually built a good German team. In time we had several German or German-speaking designers, client service managers and others. My secretary, Helga, was German. Dr Rudi Beck, a Czech long domiciled in Britain who speaks German, was both a friend and consultant to us; he did a lot of work in Germany.

In Frankfurt his colleague was a Dr Helmut Laux. He and Rudi were interested in two-way communications. Rudi had developed ways to improve communications between a company and its divers audiences. One client was the Dresdner Bank. Rudi had visited branches, gone to the teller behind the counter and said he wanted to invest 300 marks. What advice would they offer? He recorded their replies. They shocked the senior management. From this, he developed a simple, desk-top flip-chart which enabled any teller to steer a customer through the options appropriate to him. With Laux he developed advertising which set out to appeal to both the rational and emotional aspects of potential customers. It was markedly forward-thinking.

Rudi had been at Shell International, in charge of what they called VMs – 'visible manifestations', or how Shell looked. (He was in Shell when their 43-acre office block on the south bank of the Thames was proposed, then the largest office block in Europe. Hearing it was to be built, he asked to be involved. He was informed curtly that the new office complex was 'not regarded as a visible manifestation of the company'.) Rudi knew the role of design even if his directors didn't. He brought the head of the Dresdner Bank in London, Dr Kurt Richebacher, in to see our work. In time, he gave us a contract to develop a new corporate identity for the bank in Germany. Then I made a mistake. This was such an exciting export order for us that I asked Dr Richebacher, by letter, whether we could announce it. By letter he said yes. A day or two later a snippet appeared in a German newspaper. Clearly, someone in the bank didn't like it, or Richebacher had appointed us without telling others. Angry and embarrassed, he cancelled the project.

Months later Rudi Beck managed to restore it. After due study, a German designer on our staff, Ulrich Haupt, created a good solution for the bank. But then he left us – he wanted to become an orchestra conductor and had been advised by Sir Adrian Boult to return to Germany where there were far more orchestras than in Britain. When we were due to present our work to the president of the Dresdner Bank, Mr Ponto (who was later murdered by the Bader-Meinhoff gang), we called Ulrich to ask if he would come back to present his work. It was always our attitude that the people who did the work should help present it. If there was praise, they should receive it. If there were questions and criticism, they were best placed to say what had been in their mind. Mind you, the designer was invariably backed up by others.

Ulrich, as a German, did very well. Our other presentation was far less successful. Our interior designers in Sweden were developing a visionary concept of a 'moneyless' bank. That is to say, a branch where transactions were done electronically or by card. I decided they should present their work at the same meeting. The night before, in a *Bierkeller*, the Swede who was to make the presentation ordered food and drinks, teased the waitress and seemed to me to speak good German. I asked him what language he would use next day (his English is excellent). 'If you speak German, why not use it?' I asked. But what works in a pub won't do in a boardroom. The Swede's work was all right, but he couldn't find the words to explain it and the whole event collapsed in confusion. The irony is that if he'd spoken in English, no one would have minded.

The moral is not to leave presentations to chance. The Brits had rehearsed, the Swedes hadn't. We'd timed Ulrich to the minute, even suggesting to him where to pause, what to stress. As a result his presentation flowed. I am sure clients recognize the care you've gone to and appreciate it. Further, such preparation is vital because it gives the client confidence. In the Swede's case, they saw the lack of preparation only too clearly. It also shows that while you should do business in the local language, there is another truth: it is better to know your stuff in the wrong language than to be ignorant in the right language.

Jan Stael von Holstein joined us. Born a Swede, he'd worked in the design business in New York as well as in London and doubtless elsewhere. A master of umpteen languages, he told me without the slightest bragging, that he believed he could pick up most languages in a few weeks. He had the ear. Certainly, his German, French, Italian and Portuguese were as good as his Swedish and English. Jan's name, too, is international. In Germany he can be Baron von Holstein. In France he can be Jean de Stael. In New York he was once called 'Johnny Stein'. Jan sold a great deal for us, then came to head our international business for a while.

Jeremy Danks, or Jeremy C. Lovitt-Danks, came into the company. He, too, is fluent in several languages – German, French, Italian, maybe others. Tall, lean, loquacious (in several languages), devoted, chaotic, loving and lovable, he looked the quintessential Englishman from the pages of Noel Coward or P. G. Wodehouse. Jeremy came to be our man in Germany. He may not have looked the German part, but his thoroughness and commitment won through.

For some time he worked from London, but he argued, rightly, that what we needed was someone on the spot, a German who would be able to open doors for us at a high level. He came across just the man. Tall, tanned, prematurely grey, beautifully dressed, he looked like Hollywood's idea of an American ambassador. Indeed, he'd spent time with the US army and spoke fluent American. We agreed terms, all was well. Then the man asked for an annual retainer to be paid in full, in advance. He'd earn commission on top. I thought it foolish to pay a comparative stranger so trustingly. But Jeremy insisted: did we trust him or didn't we? How could a man of his background be less than scrupulous? So we paid in advance. That was the last Jeremy, or any of us, saw of him.

Jeremy, however, was one of us. We trusted him absolutely. He set up a small office in Frankfurt. Then he asked for a car, because in Germany, he explained irrefutably, you travel everywhere by *Autobahn*. So we gave him a car. Two years later he shipped it back to England unused. Why unused? Because Jeremy couldn't drive. We'd never thought to ask him!

Huge Hoechst

Jeremy, working with Jan Stael von Holstein and me, won a large programme of work with Farbwerke Hoechst AG, as it was then called. The sale took two years at least. We identified Hoechst as a prospect on two counts. First, the long-time chairman, under whom nothing would change, retired. (He was so set in his ways he always signed letters in green ink, the exclusive right of *Ober-kommando*, unmentionable in recent times.) A younger man took his place. Second, this company was widely criticized for polluting the countryside. Hoechst is one of the largest chemical companies in the world, with the usual spread of activities, from producing basic chemicals through to developing paint, pharmaceuticals and cosmetics. Its sprawling factory dominates the village of Hoechst, on the outskirts of Frankfurt. Over Hoechst hung a pall of yellow smoke.

The company had spent millions to reduce such pollution (it made a film called *The Yellow Flame* about its efforts), but still it was thought to be a heavy, dirty, autocratic, insensitive, uncaring, anti-social giant. That wasn't quite fair, but there it was. We conducted a thorough, Europe-wide study of attitudes to the chemical industry generally and to this company in particular. That first part is impor-tant: our attitudes to any company are inevitably influenced by what we think of its industry as a whole. You have to understand one to come to terms with the other. The strategy report we prepared was, I believe, the most thoughtful and far-reaching we produced.

Though several of us, not least our information department, con-tributed to the report, Jeremy Danks was in charge of it. He always works up to the very last minute and then a bit longer, improving, adding, improving some more. Knowing this, I'd said to Jeremy, 'Stop writing the report a full week before we present it. Give yourself a week to put it together attractively, so that people can find their way around it easily and enjoy what they read.' Ha. I arrived in Frankfurt the night before the report was to be presented. There was Jeremy, in his hotel room, with sheets of the report spread in a wide semi-circle around his perch on the edge of the bed. He was still adding and altering.

Never mind. The presentation next morning was very well received. Our analysis was accepted. For the meeting we had also prepared a proposed work programme for the next stages. That was something we'd learnt. It is very easy to just concentrate on the job in hand. When all goes well and the client says, 'Fine, what happens now?' often you can only extemporize. You have to go away and come back some weeks later with a programme. It's better to be able to answer the question on the spot.

Striking presentation

When our strategy document was approved, we set up three creative teams to think of design solutions. Geoff Gibbons led one, Werner Strauli another, Kevin McGurk the third. We targeted each slightly differently. One would be rather more conservative, bearing in mind that Hoechst was a huge and conservative company. A second would express the human values we wanted to inculcate and communicate within the company and outside. A third would be more advanced, high-science, modern. The solutions were marvellous. Then the sketches had to be turned into good presentation material. Part of the presentation was to be on boards – you print the design on transfers, then rub them down, to get a perfect finish.

As ever, though the designers had been thinking and working for weeks, they left too little time for the studio people, who create the artwork, to do their job.

'It was a disaster,' recalls Kevin McGurk.

Waiting later and later for the work to be completed, Jeremy Danks had had to catch the last plane from London. The presentation boards were packed in three large portfolio bags, too large to go in the aircraft's cabin. When the two men arrived in Frankfurt, the bags didn't appear. They were not on the carousel. It was 2 a.m. and the presentation to Hoechst was to start at 9 a.m. that morning. They would have nothing to present. They were wearing jeans, had no suitable clothes, not even a toothbrush between them.

'Was that the disaster?' I asked Kevin. No. at 3 a.m. fortune smiled on them. Their luggage, and the black bags, had arrived, somehow, on a long-haul jet bound for South Africa.

Being the professionals they are, Jeremy and Kevin agreed to meet at 8 a.m., an hour before the presentation to run through it. Their hearts sank when they opened the bags to rehearse. 'It looked as if the designs had been through a spin-drier,' Kevin told me. Because the studio had had too little time, they had used a fast-drying thinner to lay down the artwork on the boards. By dawn it had flaked off. 'Ah, that was the disaster,' I said. 'No,' said Kevin, 'that wasn't it.' It was now 8 a.m. Jeremy, the German speaker, rushed off to find some coloured pens. He found an art shop. He banged on the closed door to wake up the owner who lived above. He bought the pens, then dashed to the hotel, where he and 'half the hotel staff' coloured in missing bits as fast as they could.

They arrived at Hoechst on time. They are good these two. To their relief, they were kept waiting. That gave them time not only to catch their breath, but also to plan where the Hoechst people should sit – not close enough to see the botched-up work. The main-board director walked in with his retinue. The presentation started. It was going quite nicely when a freak wind began to roar outside. A horizontal window banged open. It hit the director on the head and knocked him out. *That* was the disaster.

The day of the disaster

Or was it? The meeting was cancelled and a new one arranged for two weeks later. Time to re-do all the boards. The next presentation was smooth as silk.

There is more to learn from Hoechst. We knew a number of middle managers, but just the one director. Within a week or two of accepting our work, he was ousted from the board. In other hands, without the understanding that had grown over the months, only pale echoes of our work survived. That was a shame. The essence of our strategy, to move the group from 'dark to light', as we put it, from being perceived as a heavy, basic chemical producer polluting nature, towards being a light, sophisticated, customer-loving company that benefits mankind, has grown more timely year by year. The design Geoff Gibbons did was very natural: puffy, white clouds on a blue sky. He said, 'We want to make the sun come out,' to escape, he meant, from the grey dourness of heavy chemicals. His allusion was lost on the audience. They looked out of the window to see what the weather was like. Geoff's design would serve them well today. You see bits of it, but not the whole-hearted expression that is necessary to shift understanding.

Work method

When you start a project you have to establish the right to present to the main board as a whole. Relying on one director can be risky, as we saw. In time we developed the now well-tried method of having two teams. One would be a small review board, to set the project up, agree its goals, monitor performance. The other would be a larger, flexible working-party charged with handling the day-to-day. A director of the client company chairs the first, a manager the second. You need both. If you work only at a high level, people below will find fifty ways to fix you. By contrast, if you work closely with whoever has to implement the programme, they become as much authors of the results as you are.

Hoechst was a good example. Thanks to Jeremy, we got on well with the middle managers. Because they trusted him and our firm, they introduced us to other parts of the group that came to us for other work.

Jeremy had the opportunity to sell our audio-visual group's work into Hoechst. But things happen to him. (Reading this it is wonderful to reflect that he was head-hunted by American Express and has had a wonderful career since.) Jeremy was to present a technique known as 'cross-fade', where you have two projectors with a fading mechanism lined up to give the same image. As the picture from one projector fades off, the picture from the other fades on. The results can be continuous and 'movie-like' if well done. Music and commentary are synchronized automatically with the slides. Unlike movies, though, you can change a slide and alter the message. To make this point, we would drop in a slide of that day's newspaper. It worked like a charm. Better still, a programme using this technique costs one-tenth of the price of a film.

Well, there is Jeremy, in his hotel room the night before, rehearsing. Very good. Except that he blew the bulbs in the projectors. That can happen, so we made a rule always to carry two spares. Jeremy blew one of them too. So first thing next morning Jeremy was again rushing around Frankfurt in desperation looking for a camera shop. Miracle, he found one and bought bulbs. He arrived in the conference room of Hoechst minutes before his show was to start, trying to line up the projectors and get the lighting right while pausing to chat to managers who, by now, were arriving. He started, but the new bulbs were less bright than the old. So the show went: *bright* image, dull image, *bright* image, dull image. Not as it should have been. Jeremy got through it and stayed friends with Hoechst, though I'm not sure we were asked to do any audio-visual work for them.

Accidents happen in the best of families. When Eric Baskerville was with Lintas he went to a mammoth Unilever presentation in New York, in a great cinema-like auditorium. The first speaker was to show slides. The lights dimmed. When the slide came on the curtains closed. When the slide went off, the curtains opened.

Persistence

See if there is anything to learn from our experience with Hoechst. One lesson is the time it took. If you are working from your main office, you can afford to wait nearly two years, but you're unlikely to tolerate a local office in which you've invested taking so long to produce results. That is a mistake. When we invest we expect too quick a payback – or at least signs of success. The key point is that our work for Hoechst was an example of international business succeeding. Notwithstanding human error – and building error if we count the broken window – we did penetrate and serve a number of the largest corporations in Germany, the heart of our long-range business plan.

We designed consumer electronic products in Germany, a number of large corporate-identity programmes for famous groups, plenty of packaging and print. None of that would have been possible when I went on my first reconnaissance trip to Cologne. It is interesting to note how we built German competence in London – for example Werner Stauli redesigned all the beer labels for Löwenbräu, the Bavarian brewer, from London.

One key ingredient of our success was consistently good service. We all felt we had to be super-efficient to counter any prejudice people might have about Britain – the land of the inefficient, it was widely considered. We had to match the service clients demand, legitimately, from their suppliers down the road. That wasn't always easy but, as I once remarked in another context, 'Never run a business to suit its administrators.'

Mullers Muhle

Mullers Muhle, a food firm in Gelsenkirchen, tested that philosophy to its limit. We redesigned all their packaging. Kevin McGurk led the project. Invariably, Mullers Muhle called for meetings to start at 9.30 in the morning. For Kevin and others who flew from London, that meant getting up at 5.30 a.m. It meant driving to Heathrow, taking the first plane to Dusseldorf, then driving for an hour through the German countryside. Because Kevin didn't want them to feel our service was less good than that of their local advertising agent, he agreed.

After the first meeting had finished, the people from one department concerned would leave and a new lot would come in. The meetings continued in this way, wave following wave, until 6 p.m. In all those hours our people were offered nothing: no coffee, no tea, no lunch. At the end of the day, tired and hungry, they'd drive back to Dusseldorf, take the plane to London and arrive home at maybe 10 p.m. or later. They did this ten times at least. On the seventh trip, Kevin bought some sandwiches at the airport. During the meeting he said, 'Excuse us, we must eat.' After that, Mullers Muhle provided lunch.

Why choose us?

The client treated us as they treated their agency in Dusseldorf. That is how it should be. But why did a German food firm come to Britain to have its packaging redesigned in the first place. Gerhard Muller, the marketing manager, wrote later: 'There were three reasons why the company came to Britain. The first was a recommendation from another German firm which had used you. Second, it was thought you had the right blend of marketing understanding and creative competence. Third, you were thought to possess all the back-up services necessary to achieve practical results quickly. In practice we found these judgements correct.'

Our work in Germany throws up another point. 1992. What's the best way to tackle it? Should you export from the centre? Do you need to establish offices everywhere or at least in your main markets? What's best? In a service business it is not easy to establish whether you have to be on the spot, to give the service customers want, or whether quality matters more. The quality comes, I am sure, from good people talking to each other, arguing about the right ways to do things. And, of course, today you often need your own infrastructure of services – in our case, as well as designers and design managers who ran projects, we needed artwork, information, financial control, and other skills.

Often offices in other countries tend to be smaller, with fewer resources and fewer senior people to bounce ideas around. Their loyalty to your ways of doing things may be less.

Despite the fact that Jeremy Danks was as committed as a person can be, I believe he performed better in Germany from London that he did when he was in Germany. It seems to me that quality is likely to be higher when it comes from the heart of a business and not from one of its arms.

Mistakes we make

Jan Stael von Holstein, who has as much experience of international business as anyone in design, believes that the best way to build offices abroad is to go into partnership with local people. I'd agree, though we tried that too. It is important to make a long-term commitment, he points out: say you'll invest for five years and stay with it. The reason he gives is TTT – things take time. Good sales, as we have seen, can take one year, two years or more to come in. In your home office you expect and allow for that. Once abroad, we become more demanding, often unreasonably. I would admit both to under-investing and to expecting results too soon.

Jan paints this picture: you decide to set up an office abroad. Where? You love France, so that is where you go. You don't ask where you are most likely to succeed. If someone says, 'The real opportunity is Greece,' you look askance. France it'll be. You try to sell there. It doesn't work. You hire a French salesperson. At first both of you are 'full of enthusiasm'. After three months there's nothing to show. 'Michel,' you ask, 'how many companies did you see? How did you approach them?' He says he can't do more. After six months, still without much to show, you decide you've made a mistake. Michel is useless. So you hire someone else and expect them to make more calls . . . Two years later, the job Michel worked on comes in. What you should do, says Jan, is be patient. And if you are not succeeding, plough more people into the job.

Breaking into a market is the hard part. How do you start? One way is to talk to the people who have used you elsewhere. The boss of Payot, the French cosmetics firm, had previously worked for Gillette. Jan von Holstein knew him from there. The boss of Eugen La Croix, a German food firm, had been a client of ours in two previous jobs in Britain. Another way, as we've seen, is to seek advice and help from embassies. A third is to meet journalists and try to interest them. A fourth is to arrange to give talks in the country. That can be a good way to widen your network, as the Albert Heijn example showed.

Without doubt, demonstrating knowledge of the potential client's industry is important. Research and rifle-fire targeting are the keys. A young Yugoslav who had spent a few months in a British design firm decided he wanted to open a design office in his country. How, he asked Jan von Holstein, should he go about it? Jan's advice was that he should spend a year identifying which companies he wanted to sell to, then find out about them – who they are, what their problems are and why they should employ a designer.

Case after case, in my experience, proves the value of this patient, thorough approach. It is a far cry from our demand for quick results.

8 Everyone's Risky Choice: France

At the end of 1988 the Chartered Society of Designers in Britain asked members whether, in view of 1992, they intended to do more work abroad. Yes, most said. Where? The country preferred above all others was France. Oh, my ears and whiskers, this book is needed.

It is easy to see why France tops the list. We learn French in school. Apart, perhaps, from America, France is the foreign country we are taught most about. We go there on holiday. We love it, and moon winters away dreaming of freshly baked croissants and *café au lait* on check tablecloths, imagining black-bereted *paysans* playing boule in sun-dappled cobbled squares. All our dreams are true. It is a glorious country. But for most of us, France is not the place to start doing business. Even Marks & Spencer lost its shirt when it opened in Paris. So have umpteen others, designers among them.

At L'Etoile in Charlotte Street I sat through lunch listening to a friend thrilling to a company his firm had just bought in France. It cost £23 million. 'I take my hat off to you,' I said. 'Of all the British companies I know in France none makes any money – and you seem to.' He glanced at me sideways, drew in his breath and said, 'Well . . . we don't actually make any money there.'

There may be three reasons. One is that in France the beginning, middle and end of the world is France. When a Frenchman was asked if he'd been to Rome, there was a pause. 'Rome . . . in Italy?' he replied. As was said of one viceroy of India (who'd been to Balliol College, Oxford), 'What he doesn't know isn't knowledge.' It is very difficult for foreigners to convince a French business that they might have something local firms lack. The idea of using people from England either strikes French businessmen as bizarre or doesn't strike them at all. Second, there is a very high level of Anglophobia, although it isn't universal. Third, it is easy in France to be cheated. I've been short-changed over a loaf of bread. It is not because French people can't count. One thing they can do is count. Nor are we the only sport. In the south of France a Parisian told me, 'You are lucky. If you're English, they'll overcharge by 10 per cent. If you are a

Parisian, it'll be 20 per cent.' I'd add, too, that French businessmen are often cleverer than we are. Perhaps they are more single-minded. Generally they are better trained and maybe money means more to them.

I say this not to be unpleasant but to urge anyone planning to work in France for the first time to beware. It is all the more ironic, therefore, that the best arrangement we made outside England was in France.

In common with everyone else and for the same reasons, our first links with another country were with France. After we'd been going no more than a year or two we marketed in Britain a newsletter called the European Packaging Digest. Our idea was to tell people in the British packaging industry what new equipment was available from other countries. The newsletter was written and produced by a friend in Paris. It was a useful thing to do, extending our name and paying its way, if no more.

Thanks to that friend, I went to Paris to give talks to packaging conferences, and spent a lot of time there. When, years later, the time came to think of working in France, there were a number of people in the firm who knew the country and spoke French well. Better, we had services that were scarcely known in France at that time. There were, perhaps, two or three serious design offices in Paris. We looked for partners, but we had no success.

The way in: big bank

Our entry to the French market came by chance, as so often happens. Bob MacLaren had used us when he was creative director of an advertising agency in Amsterdam. He moved to Paris and through him we met Crédit Lyonnais, one of Europe's largest banks. That became a wonderful job. A team of our designers, with a design manager, toured France to look at bank branches. Nice, Antibes, Cannes and St Tropez seemed to take them an inordinate amount of time but, we said, why not; they work hard all year.

Earlier in my career I had photographed bank branches in the United States and three loyal citizens had called the police. We learned from that. In France when we photographed a bank we posed a fashion model in front of it. To the passerby, it was just another picture for a fashion magazine.

Crédit Lyonnais was a good, big client, just the name to open other doors. We worked hard at it. Philippe Rasquinet, by now handling

France for us as well as Belgium, penetrated L'Abbaye et La Paix, an insurance company. He was dealing with the president who, it was clear, had decided to use us. Philippe asked me to go with him to close the sale. I wish I hadn't.

We'd agreed the work programme, everything was going smoothly. Then the president, sitting behind a Louis XV desk, asked me, as the sort of formality one has to go through, how much it would cost. We were ready. Philippe and our financial people had worked it our carefully beforehand and Philippe had told me. I gave the figure. Philippe looked alarmed. The president just looked. Speaking in French, I'd added a nought by mistake: instead of 400,000 francs, I'd said 4 million. Philippe was too surprised or polite to correct me. At the time there seemed no going back. So that was the end of that – months of patient effort had been thrown away.

If a moral is needed: conduct money talks in your own language or leave them to a native speaker.

Several of us tried hard in France, no doubt because we loved the country. We had some success, but not enough. It was tough going. Plainly, we didn't know how to persuade French businesses to use us. After years of working in other countries we thought it was straigh-

How to photograph a bank

forward, but, for us at any rate, it wasn't. For a while we employed an agent, a door-opener, a Comtesse de Quelquechose, who did quite well. She introduced us to a few heads of large companies, but on the whole we didn't get far.

For years, we tried to get into that huge glass conglomerate, St Gobain Pont à Mousson. At a lowly level we were well-received. They could see we had something to offer. After endless present-ations and lunches, the great day came: we were to meet a director. We'd set up the projector, our slides, in French, like all our printed matter, were ready. We had studied the company and thought we knew where to strike.

In bustled a short, plump, busy-looking man. My French was good enough to catch what he said: 'Why am I here?' he asked an aide. 'We have nothing to learn from the English.' We pressed on. He was so offensive at one stage I said to Philippe, in English, 'C'mon, let's go, this is a waste of time,' and moved to pack up. The director under-stood (he had pretended not to speak English until then) and quietened down. But though people lower in St Gobain continued to try, nothing came of it.

At that time, too, in the seventies, design was less understood. People couldn't see what it could do for them. Big French companies were more autocratic than we were used to. They weren't very interested in communicating with their workers, or anyone else other than their customers – and they used advertising agencies for that.

Hot prospect

At another talk I gave in Paris, two men in the audience gave me their cards and asked if I would go to see them. They came from a firm called Editions de Vaillant. They published weekly children's comics, one of which, *PIF*, had the biggest circulation in France. What was remarkable was that every week they attached a new product to the cover, as a premium. Their ability to find, develop and produce things cheaply in huge numbers was astonishing. They wanted us not only to invent and develop new products for them, but also to suggest a forward strategy for the company.

It was exciting. Three of us went to Paris. We studied the company, interviewing various people, including the company secretary. I asked him who owned the firm. He puffed at his cigarette then replied, '*un holding.*' Stupidly, I persisted: 'But who owns that?' He puffed more, then lit another cigarette from the first. The company was owned by the Communist party. The idea that the Communist party should own the biggest publisher of children's comics in France shook us. Think of the opportunity for subversion. If that sounds alarmist and you think we were melodramatic, remember that not long ago the left was rampaging through Europe.

By mistake, I multiplied the fee by ten

I asked Philippe to go through as many comics as he could, looking for signs. The most sinister he could find was Robin Hood. None the less, back in the hotel we decided we didn't want to play. Although we'd incurred a good deal of expense, we withdrew from the contract. The company was annoyed. They said they had told us who owned them at the beginning. Perhaps they had. Perhaps my inadequate French had missed it.

The good way

As well as being a country we enjoyed, France is an important market. Paris is a gateway to other Francophone and Latin countries. Try as we did, from London it was difficult to make a dent there – we knew we had to have a local office.

Having worked consistently with us for ten years and having proved his grit one hundred times over, Philippe Rasquinet, together with his wife Anne-France, decided that it was time for them to move back to the Francophone world. They went to Paris. With a French management consultant and two experienced designers, one British the other American, Philippe formed a design company. Because he is loyal, but also because his company needed what we could offer, they used our name and our case histories, and so became part of our international network. This suited us both: Philippe and his colleagues wanted their own firm. We wanted an office in Paris without the worries we'd experienced before.

We worked out a franchise arrangement, perhaps without precedent in our field. In exchange for the help we gave, we received a small proportion of their overall revenue. How they spent money, what profit they made, whether they would reveal or try to hide it, became no concern of ours. It was in our interest to help them grow, but if they wanted to drive Maseratis or eat every night at Le Tour d'Argent (none did), we could still sleep easy. It was a good arrangement. We continued to co-operate closely. With his own background and our case histories. Philippe was soon working for banks and other large companies. Counting on our international spread, he could compete for and win work from international groups.

The five ingredients which made this franchise arrangement work were: one, we knew and trusted each other. Two, the French company followed our way of doing things (the American had come from Raymond Loewy's office, the Englishman from Fitch; we all worked in much the same way). Three, their work is excellent – remember the trouble we'd had in Sweden when standards varied between offices. Four, we needed each other and were complementary. Five, we kept contacts live, information between us flowed rapidly and regularly.

That office in Paris has done wonderfully. It is now among the most important, perhaps the largest, in France. Its success proves that you can franchise professional services. If the right conditions are met they can work well. See, too, how many of the heartaches vanish. Misunderstandings occur, but, as long as you need and respect each other, they are not lethal.

Sadly, after I'd left the company a successor made an elementary, even insulting mistake. He went to Paris and offered Philippe and his colleagues an ultimatum: sell a majority of shares to the home company, or leave. After his long commitment, Philippe was shocked. Unsurprisingly, he told the clumsy predator where to go. There is a lesson in that, too.

9 Across the Atlantic: The United States

As schoolboys in England during the war we laughed at the Yanks. What was wrong, it was said, was that they were 'over-sexed, over-paid and over here'. (The Yanks apparently replied, 'The British are undersexed, underpaid and under Eisenhower.') Still, they *were* over here, many as brave and kind as man could hope for. Ever since I have entertained the belief that Anglo-American partnership is as natural as breathing. With more experience I know this is not always so, but it remains my position. It is an affair of the heart started long ago.

Philip Marsh was the 'schoolie' (education officer) in my regiment. He had been evacuated during the war to an ivy-league school in America. Huddled in cold barracks, rain streaking down the blackened windows, he regaled us with sun-blest stories. (Tall, broad-shouldered, fair, he once got a summer job lying by a pool. His employer thought his good looks would attract custom.) America seemed a wonderland. But, he sighed, it was impossible to get there. First, you needed a visa and there was no hope of getting one. Second, if you did, you could only take £5 out of England. I made a five-shilling bet with him I'd manage it. I then found out that if you were going to Canada you could go via New York.

Before I set off I went to see an old lady who lived in my village. Plump, always dressed in black with a high lace collar, she wore around her neck a gold pendant, shaped like a fan, with a glass face. In it was gold dust her father had panned in the second Californian gold rush. Born in England, she had grown up in America in *Gone with the Wind* style, with land, servants, horses. Hearing I was going to New York, she warned me severely to avoid robbers in city hotels who would entertain you with fine words downstairs while companions rifled luggage in your room, and she gave me advice that still fits now. 'Always remember the world is your erster.' That was her way of saying oyster. She thought the English don't know that well enough. She took her own advice even if I found it hard to do so. One day I saw her hobbling with a stick towards the railway station. She was going to Bath to look at a church she'd read about. 'You're wonderful, Miss Bamber,' I said. 'Well,' she replied 'you gotta do sump'n. Otherwise you jest sit at home and rot like an old cabbage.' She was eighty-six at the time.

First impressions

I am lucky; I first saw New York from the deck of a ship. In the early morning the towers of Manhattan rose through the mist, magical, ethereal. It was a sight never matched from the air.

I had joined the English-Speaking Union. I went to their offices in New York. A woman looked at me. 'You're English,' she said. 'You haven't any money. Come back at two o'clock.' I did. Without a word she thrust a paper in my hand. It was an address in the 'eighties', overlooking Central Park, the townhouse of a lady said to be the fifth-richest person in America. By her breakfast plate each morning were two typed sheets of paper. One listed her agenda for the day, the other gave a summary of the news and reviews of books and plays. Each day she gave me tickets for plays – the Oliviers in Anthony and Cleopatra was one. That is how I first saw the United States.

In January, when the air is crisp and the sky bright blue, New York is at its most handsome. I wandered around Times Square when it *was* Times Square: smoke blew from a Camel ad, Budweiser horses tossed their heads, news in lights sped around and around the high 'motorama'. I saw Forty Second Street when it was Damon Runyon land, not the filthy drug alley of today. I wondered at the dog-in-a-mink-jacket wealth of Park Avenue, steam rising from vents in the road, bumping yellow taxis, and policemen as Irish as they were said to be. All the stereotypes were there, living in colour before my young eyes. If some of my images of America remain as innocent as an old movie, those first glimpses are among the reasons.

Aged 22 I had had a honeymoon in New York. My wife and I watched skaters at the Rockefeller Center on Christmas morning, and danced to Guy Lombardo and his Royal Canadians at the Roosevelt by night.

As a journalist I later interviewed leaders of the American design world and got to know Raymond Loewy, Walter Margulies, Henry Dreyfuss, Frank Gianninoto (under his name on his writing paper he had printed 'Johnny Noto'), Walter Dorwin Teague and others. Teague had held the Boeing account for twenty years or more. When he died the magazine *Industrial Design* invited readers to sum him up. Students won the prize. 'Walter Dorwin Teague,' they wrote simply,' was big league.'

One day a salesman from Lippincott & Margulies, a big New York design office, came to the magazine I worked on in Canada. He wanted us to write about a job his firm had just done. We got to know each other. He always talked big, but I found it amusing. 'Don't talk about the war,' he'd say, 'I was in the OAS.' (The OAS was the American cloak and dagger operation in Europe, later to become the CIA). 'Yes,' he admitted another day, 'I like pictures. My wife and I have a few Renoirs and Dufys . . .'

Then he invited my wife and me to New York. We were met at the airport by a Filipino manservant driving a Cadillac. Our host put us up in a good hotel, then asked us to dinner. He and his beautiful wife, a well-known actress, lived in a chic brownstone house. In a glass display cabinet decorations were laid out. One was an English order of knighthood he almost certainly didn't own, although he did claim to be the eighteenth duke of something Spanish. And there were the pictures.

After dinner his wife took mine off to the Waldorf, ruffling through a line of mink coats to find one suitable for her to wear. The man and I sat down. After a moment he touched a button. A Dufy slid aside to reveal a television set, already on, showing a wrestling match.

Wanting to return his hospitality, I invited him and his wife to dinner. Since he knew New York, perhaps he could suggest somewhere. I'd only heard of two restaurants in New York: Sardi's and the 21. Being a young journalist with very little money, my blood ran cold when he suggested Sardi's. Still, there was nothing for it.

When my wife and I arrived at the restaurant they wouldn't let us in. How it changed when I gave his name. We were swept to a large round table in the middle of the room. In one corner, rather near the service entrance, was Noel Coward. Dotted about were other stars. The more we ate, the more ashen the food tasted. It got worse. Friends of our guests arrived and sat with us. No, no, they wouldn't stay . . . well, perhaps they would just have a little lobster . . . how kind. When the bill came partial relief swept over me: I could just pay it. All was well. Only later did I realize that the man we'd invited must have paid the lion's share privately. It was both a tactful and generous act.

Later that man moved to Bucks County, to a turreted chateau shipped, it was said, brick by brick from France. He invited me to stay. The house was set in a great park with a lake where we shot arrows at a target.

I mention him because he later became my boss. He bought into a design office in New York and recruited me to create its Canadian office. While I never believed his yarns, I enjoyed them and liked him. Senior people in the company were more cautious. They hired detectives to check his background. Of course, none of it matched, but he was always too quick with answers to be exposed.

Later still I read a law case in England. By chance, I knew all the characters. A pretty socialite had married a wealthy young man, who was killed in an air crash. When his will was read, she found she had been left one shilling and two photographs of herself in the nude. My former boss, described in *The Times* as a 'Mexican banker', which he certainly wasn't, was accused and convicted at the Old Bailey, of forging the will.

While I worked for that design office in New York, this man urged me to sell the services of the company's home economics department. What it did, my friend said, was to pick up old country recipes from county fairs, then work out how they could be made by large packaged food firms. Interested, I asked to meet people in the home economics department. For months nothing happened. 'Oh, no,' I was told, 'their work is very confidential.' One day the founder of the design office invited me to lunch. To my surprise, we pushed through the door labelled 'Home Economics Department'. It was his pied-à-terre in New York. A large beaming lady called Atlanta cooked us a delicious omelette . . . and that was the end of being asked to sell country recipes.

My first sale in America

Since those days I have been to New York many times, attending conferences, giving talks, buying firms, trying to sell. Even so our first sale in the United States happened by accident.

I'd been to the World's Fair in Osaka and was on my way home. From Japan I flew across the Pacific to the West Coast, then over to New York. I reached the hotel in Manhattan at about 5.30 p.m. on a Wednesday. There was a message from my secretary in London. Would I call Michael Berkes in Chicago, she asked. Who was he? Heaven alone knew. Still, I rang. 'You got my letter?' he asked. 'That's marvellous. I only posted it in Chicago, on Monday evening . . . Well, what do you think? Are you interested?'

'Tell me more,' I stalled. It turned out we had met on an aircraft flying from Sweden some years before when I'd told him about corporate-identity work we were doing for banks. Now he, a management consultant, had a bank client in need of design help. The bank was in Worcester, Massachusetts. Would I like to meet the president of the bank?

'Sure,' I replied.

'When could you manage?'

'Anytime,' I said. 'Tomorrow morning?'

Michael Berkes was impressed, but then curious. 'Where are you calling from?' he asked.

'New York.'

'God,' he burst out, 'that's what I call service.' He assumed I'd received the letter in London and hopped on a plane at once. Here I was in New York, two days after he'd written. I don't know if I ever disabused him of this idea. Next day we met in Worcester. The bank president, no less impressed by this amazing service, employed us.

Changing Worcester

All I knew of Worcester, Massachusetts, was that Jung and Freud came here from Vienna to talk at the same symposium. They quarrelled on the boat and, after giving their papers, never spoke to each other again.

Worcester is a university town about an hour west of Boston. The bank, then Worcester Five Cents Savings Bank, had maybe six branches in Worcester and local townships. I asked if I could conduct a photo-survey of them, inside and out. Two vice-presidents and a large car were made available. We drove from branch to branch. Two things happened: one, three good citizens phone the police to warn them someone was taking pictures of banks, and two, I forgot to put a film in my camera. Shamefacedly I confessed and we repeated the process the next day. That aside, the job went very well. Ron Haselton, the president, is very driving and imaginative. Tom Zocco, his senior vice-president, accepted me even though he and his wife thought it bizarre to be using foreigners.

In my analysis I predicted that the bank's clientele would alter from local farmers and tradespeople, the traditional core of New England, to a new generation of people moving into the hi-tech businesses along Route 128. For them, associations with 'five cents' were old-fashioned. We proposed, and the bank accepted, a change of name. Geoff Gibbons created a very good and modern design which was applied widely. The service he provided was stunningly good.

Haselton, who later wrote that our association was 'a high point' in their bank's development, came to London a couple of times. He'd never been before. The day after he arrived we had lunch at Antoine's, a fish restaurant in Charlotte Street. He saw smoked salmon on the menu. 'I haven't had smoked salmon for twenty years,' he said. When the food came he groaned. 'You know why I haven't eaten smoked salmon for twenty years?' he asked. 'I don't like it.'

When our work for the Worcester bank was finished, Ron Haselton introduced us to the National Association of Savings Banks. They commissioned work from us which Jan Stael von Holstein handled.

The wonderful lesson

Working for that bank taught me something of fundamental importance. I asked Haselton why he had chosen the management consultants he had. They were fine, but so were many in America. 'Ah,' he replied, 'these people are specialists in banking.' He didn't choose those consultants because they were the best in the world (although they may be), the nearest, which they weren't, or the cheapest. He picked them because he believed they understood his business.

That one sentence changed the shape of our company. From then on we started to focus on a few key industries and to understand them. In time, companies used us for just that reason. Of course, the policy became self-fulfilling. The more we worked in a few key industries, the more we understood them and the more compelling evidence we gathered to demonstrate that we understood each client's particular problems. Time and again we won work this way.

Playing golf one day in Massachusetts, I asked the Chicago consultants if they really were specialists in banking. One laughed. 'All we're specalists in is having a folder marked Banking Division.' Tut, tut.

Big or small, the problem's the same

We'd worked for British–American Tobacco in London off and on for years. Their head offices on Millbank were the legal headquarters of over 100 companies. We were asked to redesign all their stationery. The brief, incredibly, was to make them look small. They didn't want people to know how big they were. The building they were in is a block surrounded by four streets, so some companies used the address of one street, others a second, others a third street and others the fourth.

Then times changed. We entered the age of the 'transparent' company. Confusion and secrecy, companies began to see, harm understanding. No exception. BAT wanted to review its corporate identity world-wide. The company is much bigger and more wide-spread than people know. They sent me to Louisville, Kentucky, where Brown and Williamson, one of their subsidiaries which sells about one-third of the tobacco in the United States, has its headquarters.

Hardly had I walked in the door when the man in charge of corporate affairs launched into me: 'We're not a colony, you know ... Queen Victoria is dead.' All I'd said was 'good morning'. I was the recipient of his pent-up anger because an executive in London had behaved tactlessly. But the blast was salutary. Managing business in other countries is a sensitive task. The scale doesn't matter; indeed, I was often struck by how similar the problems of whales and minnows can be.

Anglo-American relations may be more complex than most. The common language and easy familiarity obscures real differences. If you are trying to sell in Germany you know people are different and take the trouble to learn the differences; you are wary and careful and thorough. Go to America, by contrast, and you feel, if not exactly at home, at least at ease, comfortable. At first, admittedly, there's the nervousness bred of believing business in the United States is super-efficient. You accept Americans' own image of themselves. Later you learn that self-delusion operates on a national scale. Business in the United States can be excellent, but it can also be, dismayingly naïve. Long words and the latest theories camouflage unsophistication. A lot of firms have bigger budgets than brains.

Yet even rumbling that doesn't seem to help much. It is a grave mistake to suppose that because you get on well and laugh at the same things, doing business in the United States is the same as doing business in Europe. It isn't. American business is based on simpler principles; their hire-and-fire attitude to staff shows that. Even financially, I have found, it is far less carefully thought through.

Having said that, business in the US shines in three ways. First is the scale, If you've got enough bombs, you can make a big splash — you don't even have to be very accurate where you drop them. Second, if you've got the money, everything works. Third, executives and boards often display more commercial courage than we are used to. They are far readier to act boldly. The English satisfaction with 'compromise', a euphemism for blunting any cutting edge until it is safe, is less often seen.

P-p-p-p-ractice

I once gave a talk about new product development to about 1,000 people crowded into the Plaza Hotel. The conference was arranged by the Advertising Association of America. One speaker had created a game to guide managers through the snakes and ladders of product development. He sold it like a fairground huckster. 'When Alexander Graham Bell invented the telephone,' he screeched, 'was that the first time he'd been in a laboratory? No. When Lindberg flew the Atlantic, was the first time he'd ever been in an aeroplane? No. When Babe Ruth hit his hundredth home run was that the first time he'd ever held a baseball bat? No. What had all these guys had?' he bellowed. 'Prrractice.' If you bought his game, he was trying to say, you'd get practice too. And practice is the way to get better. Advice for us.

The British Information Service, which introduced me to the organizers of that conference, was one of several British government agencies in the United States there to help British people do business.

A model story

When you are selling services, of course, the hard part is to convince anyone in the United States that it is sensible to employ you from three thousand miles away. It can be done. This story is almost a model.

Rudi Beck came to see me. An old friend and former consultant, he was now much involved in new techniques of what he called 'interactive communications'. With a partner in New York he was working for the world's largest insurance brokers, Marsh & McLennan. Dominant in the United States, MarshMac, as we soon called it, owned big insurance brokers in a number of other countries. Rudi said the company had set up a team to appoint corporate-identity specialists. A list of twelve American firms to choose from had been drawn up. Would we be interested to compete for the business? We would.

With his help, we thought about MarshMac a lot. Our information department gathered a great deal of relevant information not just about insurance but also about banks, the stock exchange and other financial institutions. We met Peter Bowring, chairman of MarshMac's British subsidiary. We gathered details of their operations in other countries and looked at their competitors. Together we attempted to forecast trends in the financial world. We then distilled thousands of words into a few paragraphs. In view of 'big bang', which occurred some years later, it is revealing to read the first two sentences of the slim folder we put together:

> The field of finance is becoming one world, a world of turmoil. Traditional barriers between activities of insurance companies, banks, mutual funds, etc., are breaking down. This turmoil creates immense opportunities for Marsh & McLennan . . .

On the first page we spoke of:

> A completely integrated, international financial and informational market-place, capable of moving money and ideas to any part of the planet in a matter of seconds . . .

Such remarks (made in 1983) were far-sighted, even visionary, at the time.

Our document was tersely written, to be scanned in a couple of minutes. We stated what we believed were MarshMac's needs. It said who we were, described our experience in the world of finance, and how we work. It described the people who would be on their team and touched on likely time and cost. Because we didn't know enough to estimate fees, we quoted those that had arisen on two recent, similar projects. The folder was completed by 'comments from our clients' and a collection of relevant case histories.

Rudi Beck vetted and approved of it. The folder was meant to show our understanding, experience and resources. Still, we were foreign, competing with excellent design offices local to MarshMac in New York. To cover that weakness, we asked one of my oldest friends, Bud Young, who'd designed many of America's most famous logos, to be our man on the spot.

Peter Cree, who headed both our corporate communications group and this project, and I flew over to meet the team charged with the task of recommending a company from among those they were interviewing.

On the plane I read the papers time and time again. Why, I kept asking, should the mighty firm use us? They had offices in other countries, our services were international. That was good. We could work in French, German, Italian and some other languages; surely none of our competitors in New York could match that. We could probably show more experience of designing for financial companies, banks and the like, than anyone else in the race. That was a strong point. And we were confident we had researched the future of financial services more imaginatively and thoroughly than our New York rivals would have done. The logic was all there. But still, I was uneasy. What was missing? An American general once said, 'There is always one more thing.' What was it? There was nothing to touch their hearts.

The idea that won

When Peter Cree, Bud Young and I entered the meeting the next morning I said, 'You must wonder why we are here. There are so many good design firms in New York. Why should you even think about using anyone from across the Atlantic?' Bull's-eye. It was clear from their faces that that was exactly what they were thinking. I let the question hang. 'Because,' I said after a pause, 'you are already the dominant insurance broker in the United States. Your future potential doesn't lie here, but in other countries . . . and we are closer to those countries, better equipped to work in them, than any New York office can be.'

We painted a picture of Marsh & McLennan increasing their position as the greatest insurance broker in the world, using our international resources to help get them there. That touched their hearts. Peter Cree could answer all their questions about our method and fees (not lower than anyone else's). Having Bud present was good too. There and then they appointed us. Peter Bowring, present at the meeting, took us to the 21 to celebrate.

I have described this sale at length because it seems to me full of lessons.

1 The initial contact. Although it was some years since Rudi had worked with us, he thought of us when this need arose. That was partly luck, although we had taken the trouble to keep him, like all our contacts, well aware of what we were doing. In sight is in mind.

2 Our homework was impeccable. Thanks to Rudi Beck and Peter Bowring, we had spoken to many people in and around the giant corporation, and we had the benefit of a really thorough information department (unique then). We'd also looked ahead to what the client's problems might be in the future.

3 We'd distilled piles of reports and clippings into a few, short words. We prepared a paper the busiest executive could read in a couple of minutes. It takes time to write as simply as that.

4 Before presenting it, we checked that report with people who knew the client company well.

5 Our presentation was framed entirely to answer questions that would be in their minds. How often, in the past, had we given presentations that were full of ourselves!

6 Peter, Bud and I were letter-perfect. We had discussed thoroughly answers to every question we could imagine them asking.

7 Having Bud there was crucial. His presence wasn't what won the job, but what stopped us losing it. Indeed, one of the directors asked us what we knew of the United States and how we could service them across the Atlantic. We had both questions ticked off.

8 It may be that the dissatisfaction I'd felt in the plane – leading to our search for a simple idea – was a factor.

The most important lesson is that winning this kind of work is a complex task, involving hard work by a number of people. Those who suppose the quality of their work will speak for itself may be right, or they may not. Winning jobs from large organizations is often more difficult than that. Other issues, quite properly, bear on the decision. If, with hindsight, I were to criticize our approach, I would say that we didn't think enough about our competitors. We guessed. It worked that time, but it might not always.

You may find it useful to analyse that sale to see what, in your view, were the decisive steps. A challenge like this is fun. Professional people who think selling is tawdry miss a lot, including work.

Compare that MarshMac story with the attitude of the so-called marketing director of a New York design office I knew. He was flying some 1,500 miles to see a prospect in the Midwest. As he rushed through the reception area I heard him shout over his shoulder, 'Anyone know what the hell this firm does?'

Decision to invest

We worked in the United States, off and on, though without consistent effort. Europe was going well for us, the US was a logical next step. After we became a public company we began to think about taking the market seriously, establishing a presence. We decided we couldn't create a company there, we'd do better to buy one already established. We pursued this in two ways: talking to anyone we knew for ideas, and searching systematically. I visited a number of design groups, getting brush-offs or vague promises (although three have since been bought by British companies).

I'd kept in touch with two men with whom I'd worked in the 1960s. They had a small package design office on Fifth Avenue. By now the principals were doyens of their industry. One was ready to retire, the other ought to have been contemplating it. Our timing might be ideal. Their work was solid. Their client list included many household names. They had excellent, hard-working staff, inhibited, I thought, by the powerful presence of their boss. Liberate them, I fancied, and the firm would take off.

I went to see the boss several times, moving him closer to the idea of selling his firm to us. He came near enough to let us meet his staff and to release his figures to us and let us discuss them with his auditors. With his wife he came to London to look at us. All went well. We made him offer after offer. I even asserted we could double his business. Still he never said 'yes', he could never quite step over that threshold. I now know he finds it difficult to decide anything, and the firm was his baby and his life.

So those efforts failed. It was a shame, although there was a sequel. Five years later, to my surprise, the boss flew from New York to see me in Boston. He said, 'When we last met you reckoned you could double our profits. I don't want that, just a 25 per cent growth next year. Can you do that for us?' He wanted me as a consultant.

I took the job with great pleasure. His was a business I knew. Besides, his office was a few yards from the Algonquin, where I loved staying. After poking around the company a lot, talking to everyone, looking at all the information I could find, I made recommendations. People worked immensely hard but in chaos, too busy to organize themselves. At a one-day presentation I demonstrated facts confirmed by their accountants in New York and mine in London: that they lost money on all their design work. The more design they did, the more money they lost. Their profits came entirely from material they bought in and sold on, such as photography. If they put their financial system in order, I calculated, their profits would increase 40 per cent in the first year. This was not to say that money is all that matters; by no means, but it was absurd and dangerous not to know where they made money and where they lost it. Nor was it fair to their good people who worked with such enthusiasm.

I'd seen the same before in Canada when I worked for a firm of product designers. They were retained to redesign some aluminium kitchenware – pots and pans. After studying them the boss, Ernest Orr, went to the client with a breath-taking discovery. 'That product must lose you money,' he announced, which wasn't bad for a designer in those days. He thought it would be a bombshell. To his dismay, the client said, 'Oh, we know. It is a loss-leader for the rest of the range.' When he came to work on it later, Ernest Orr found the rest of the range lost money too.

Learning from that we were always very careful to analyse every job we did. We minded less about losing money on a project if we knew about it. We hated not knowing. That is good practice generally and essential for anyone doing business abroad, where costs can multiply dizzily.

That New York design office was a good example of a company so committed to providing good service that it never had time to look at the market, look at competitors, or think where it was going. Its judgements were invariably made without knowledge. For example, because they had no knowledge of their competitors' fees, their hourly rates were well below average. The president of Coca Cola had written to ask them to visit him. For three months they'd been too busy to reply.

To California

After that effort to buy a company we knew failed, Kevin McGurk said he'd come across a design office in Orange County, south of Los Angeles, worth talking to. The founding partners were ready to sell their business because they were besotted by an invention which would make their fortune: 3-D television.

The idea of being in on some wonderful new technology from Silicon Valley intrigued us. I flew to John Wayne airport. The principals showed me around their firm. Their designers had an enviable amount of space, working in a generous, light, modern building.

The work was all right, but not special. Not much there, I thought. But maybe the 3-D television would make up for it. With great pride and excitement they showed it to me. To get the 3-D effect the viewer had to keep his or her head still. A bracket was provided for the purpose. Can *you* see the housewives of America putting their heads in a bracket to watch telly? Yet the founders had already raised several million dollars to put into the project, and were ready to sell the design business to raise more.

Should we buy the office, where, I asked myself, would their interest lie? Helping to build the design company with us, or trying to make their 3-D television work? Just in case my board was interested, I did agree terms that afternoon. Mercifully, the board took my advice and abandoned the idea.

Trouble and triumph

We bought a market-research firm in New York and started another. The latter was a great success, the former not. The reason for failure is worth describing.

The firm we bought was chosen by carefully analysing research yearbooks and other data. It had two partners. One was a hot-shot Third Avenue salesman, lean, nervous, exciting, demanding, a go-getter. By himself, we'd have said 'no'. You need more than selling. You need some calmness and thoughtfulness in a business, gravitas. That was provided by the other partner. An academic, he taught market research in the evenings in a local college and developed new, sophisticated techniques for conducting market research. Together they formed a strange alliance that worked. After plenty of talk, terms were agreed by our research people in London. Then, at a very late stage and to his obvious embarrassment, the 'salesman' partner decided to go his own way. His wife felt 'bad vibes' about me, he explained. Then we made the fatal error. Instead of crying off, we went forward with half the partnership, the academic. An agreeable man, he had no aggression or imagination whatever. He just floundered. We sent top research people from London to help and I went a number of times. But none of our advice stuck.

The fatal flaw had been pointed out to us years before by Peter Lewis, a friend and one-time non-executive director. He'd warned that when you're doing a negotiation, completing the deal can come to seem more important than the quality of the deal. We knew that so well we called it 'the Lewis effect'. Yet see what we did in New York.

The second market-research company we started was different. Qualitative, psychologically based research was the fastest-growing, most profitable part of the whole industry. With Sue Robson, we'd done wonderfully in London. So we replicated that. We found a marvellous, highly committed psychologist, very experienced and forceful. We simply invested in her. Her firm grew very well, though it wasn't long before we made the mistake of asking her to be involved in the other, ailing business. That is another thing to avoid: letting bad firms drag down good ones.

With great skill the man who became my successor acquired the second-largest design office in the United States, based in San Francisco – all for paper. It was a $7 million share exchange, believed to be only the second that had happened across the Atlantic.

I thought that office was 'a bridge too far' for us. San Francisco is a long way, further still, mentally. Although I voted against the acquisition, there was much to be said for it. Undoubtedly it achieved our goal of becoming an important player in the United States. Our complementary market-research offices in New York gave the Californians a base on the east coast. They also had a fledgling office in Tokyo, of growing interest to us. I cannot say what the present position is, although for many far-sighted British companies, investing in the United States, with its fluctuating dollar, has done no good at all to results. In the long run, though, the strategy must be right.

Name strategy

Those companies in the US each kept their own name, which makes acquisition easier. But that benefit must be weighed against the increasingly important task of building a global identity. That does not apply to all businesses, but it is relevant to companies providing sophisticated services to senior management. McKinsey is a good example. Having one name that speaks for consistent quality wherever it is seen is likely to be the best way for service companies to compete in the next decades. The problem is more subtle than a few lines suggest. Local sensibilities will remain for a long time. People in the United States, local residents as well as employees, make it plain that they dislike foreign (often British) companies acquiring their industries. I've found the same in other countries, yet the inexorable needs of global marketing will force some accommodation between local office and foreign parent.

Selling from London

Another American example from my company highlights the issue. While we had a large design firm on the west coast and two research companies in New York, one new-product development company in London, led by Kevin McGurk, carried out major assignments there. The ability to persuade large American corporations to have their new products created in London, then to satisfy them, is a pinnacle of international business success. But whether our own companies in America benefitted at all, even by reputation, is not known.

We did millions of dollars' worth of work for Kimberly-Clark in the United States, from London. I asked Kevin how he got the job. The story started, he told me, with work he did for Van den Bergh's, a Unilever subsidiary, in London. We developed packaging from Freshmill, a part-baked bread. Lloyd Hughes from McCann's, Van den Bergh's advertising agency loved our imaginative thinking. He was then head-hunted by Kimberly-Clark in Britain. They want to launch nappies in the UK. How do you launch nappies? They needed a unique idea. 'Talk to McGurk,' Lloyd Hughes said.

Our relationship grew from that. Kimberly-Clark spent £250,000 with us, so much that the chief executive in the US came to London to see what they'd spent the money on. At the end of the present- ation he said, 'I want that young man [Lloyd Hughes] in America.' His job: 'To put new ideas into our companies.' With Lloyd Hughes there and with the blessing of the chief executive, Kevin went back and forth to Kimberly-Clark in the US for years.

In the US, too, Kevin developed new products for Duracell. We used to smile. At that time design circles in England were con- stantly, and properly, praising a range of torches Nick Butler had designed for Duracell. We never mentioned, and haven't until now, our huge involvement with Duracell in the United States.

That job started as the result of a mailing Kevin sent out, Duracell in Britain responded. They came to see us. To demonstrate our way of thinking, Keven showed work we had done for Beecham which had never been used. Duracell liked it. They wanted us to adapt it to suit them . . . at our cost. This was not our usual way at all, but Kevin agreed. We'd modify the work, if Duracell would pay to research it. They did. Customers liked what they saw. That led to £250,000 worth of work in the UK. Then Kevin had to present it to the parent company in the United States. It led to over £2.5 million worth of work. By then we had an advanced micro-electronics design company in Cambridge, which earned the bulk of the fees, though Kevin's group earned 30 per cent for project management.

The point is that sometimes you have to play a hunch (modifying work for nothing, in this case). However big you get, Kevin McGurk believes, 'you mustn't lose that entrepreneurial drive.'

10 Global Strategy: South-east Asia

The first time you fly into Hong Kong you get a fright. The aircraft roars too low over the washing-lines of Kowloon. The runway, jutting into the bay, seems half the right size. Around you is sparkling water, ahead the hill of Hong Kong island, windows in its towers glinting in the bright sun.

On my first visit, years ago, the place bustled with an endless sea of busy people. Junks plied the harbour past moored warships of the Royal Navy. Rickshaws jogged in and out of the dense traffic. People were everywhere, crouched cooking on the pavement, hanging chickens outside shops, piling silks on stalls, chatting in doorways, pushing on to the Star Ferry. Beyond Connaught Square, by the club, a cricket match was being played. Behind it, in wonderful juxtaposition, a vast portrait of Chairman Mao hung the length of the Bank of China building. The air was hot and heavy and sweet.

I was in the Orient: the steamy, overgrown, polyglot East of Somerset Maugham and Graham Greene; the East of rumpled white suits, sampan hats and Sadie Thompson. Much has changed since then. Multi-national banking, Toyota trucks and TV, Sony Walkmans and westernization have ironed out the East. The relentless drive of the clever Hong Kong Chinese has created such wealth that once I wrote to a friend, 'This place makes New York look like a sleepy and rather old village.'

Several times I've given talks, taken part in seminars and visited clients in Hong Kong and Singapore. Working for European firms, a number of us had been to Kuala Lumpur, Sri Lanka, Indonesia and elsewhere. Everywhere, the energy and commitment, the speed and inevitability of growth could be felt. We wanted to be there. We didn't look for instant pay-back from South-east Asia, a mistake too often made. We just wanted to install something and let it grow naturally so that, in time, as the market grew, we would be well placed for the future.

Lintas, Unilever's advertising agency, provided the first important opportunity. Bob MacLaren, for whom we'd worked both in Amsterdam and in Paris, wanted us to help their local companies in the East. The old problem soon emerged: how do you provide the quality Unilever is used to, from thousands of miles away? Leg-work was the first answer. David Bush, head of our packaging group, rushed back and forth, with mounting success. Soon several designers were travelling too. One project led to another. Their quality of service and work was high. Every package they designed was tested in the market together with existing products and the designs of competitors. Time after time ours won.

After they had done three projects in the Far East for Unilever, our packaging group in London wrote to sixty multinational companies there. They got the names from directories or embassies. Twenty-five firms said they would see us. Bill Goodenough, who followed up, says he had 'three meetings a day for six weeks'. His effort led to one job in Thailand, two in Singapore, one in the Philippines, one in Malaysia.

Taking it in turns, our designers went to service them, trying to group visits into four trips a year, when they would be away for three or four weeks. But that service is hard to sustain.

The snag is this: if you work from London you don't know enough about the market; air fares and hotel bills make you expensive, and you are slower than local people. If, by contrast, you set up a local office, you won't have the 'critical mass' of skills you need to design well, so your standards wouldn't be what clients expect of you. For years that conflict bemused us.

One day I talked to a friend who worked for one of the large law practices in London. He had just returned from Korea. He told me time zones were such that he could draft a contract with his client during the day, send it in the evening to financial printers in London who would print the contract overnight and send it back. My friend would deliver the printed contract to his astonished client next morning. How, I asked, could documents be sent across the world so quickly? The answer was *fax*, a new word at this time.

We saw the potential at once. With fax it would be possible, we thought, to take a brief locally in the Pacific, whiz it to London together with pictures of local competitors' products and ideas for the local conditions. With this information, designers in London could do initial creative work, then fax it back. Any revisions could be handled the same way. The finished artwork, to the highest standard, could follow. No time would be lost, top quality would be maintained.

The Pacific basin

Our first line of thought was to open an office in Hong Kong. I talked to several eminent Chinese businessmen who happily blended inherited wealth with extreme acumen, drive and Harvard educations. Another friend there was Eric Waterhouse, whom I'd met when we worked for Trust House Forte in London. Eric was now running the Mandarin hotels. (Eric had been based in Hong Kong as a Royal Marine. In the mess one day, his colonel, doing a crossword puzzle, asked no one in particular the French word for something. Eric, by chance, knew it. Weeks later Eric was posted to serve with a French regiment in Vietnam. 'Why me?' he asked. 'The Colonel says you speak French,' was the reply.)

Despite our friendly contacts in Hong Kong, we decided to establish our office in Singapore. Why? We thought the Hong Kong orientation was towards China and the United States, rather than to other countries in the Pacific basin. Singapore seemed to us the epicentre, the natural focus of many Asian countries. Bill Goodenough, who developed sustained business in a number of cities throughout the area, said recently that the decision was 'absolutely right'.

Bill and his wife went to Singapore to open our office. They spent two nights in a hotel, then moved into an empty flat. Within six weeks the office was furnished, staffed and working. After a few months, during which the fax system with London worked perfectly, two things happened. First, the flow of work from Unilever companies (our core business) dried up. We had simply done all there was to do for the time being. Second, the exchange rate swung against us. It became uneconomic to do the creative work in London and then fax it out. So Bill had to build his own creative staff.

How did he tackle this? He looked for Singaporeans who were working in the design world in London, then paid them to return home. 'The biggest difficulty in opening a local office', says Goodenough, 'is to sustain quality.' With these experienced designers he was able to do so. In addition, two or three designers went out from our London office every year for up to three months. That was an imaginative and generous policy by the people in London. How much easier to have said 'no'! In practice, the policy enriched the experience of the people who went, gave a fillip to the office in Singapore, and, as designers returned, added something to the creative pulse, and job satisfaction, of the company as a whole.

Some of the markets in the Pacific basin are large (Indonesia is as

big as France, it is said), but there tends not to be an oligarchy of
leading companies in each sector, as we would expect here. That
means it is easy to find who the big players are. They are few in each
market, and even monopolistic. You have to change your methods to
succeed, as Bill did, in the Pacific basin. Almost all our work in Europe,
for example, was for public companies. In the East companies are
mostly privately owned. The worry was: who decided in those firms?
Bill recounts that often he would sit in a reception area all day waiting
to find out. When he met the principal he often won work, but it was
cyclical. They would give him a job, things would go well, then they'd
complain it was expensive. So next time they would go somewhere
cheaper. Nine months later, the company would come back.

Attitudes to fees were new, too. We worked for a bank. Bill got a
photographer to take a picture of the building. Next year, he was
asked to take another picture, this time of a bank four storeys
smaller. The client was dismayed to find himself charged the same
fee. A smaller building should command a smaller fee, he thought.
Most of our work in South-east Asia was done, on the insistence of
the client, for a fixed fee. Because there may be modifications no one
can foresee, this is not the best way. Still, we adapted. The office in
Singapore always made money, a tribute to Bill Goodenough. He
stayed three years, then returned to London for another job in the
firm. People he hired for the office in Singapore are still there. It is a
success story.

With hindsight it is clear we didn't back up the office as much as we
might have done. For example, we almost never sold our ability to
design to a high standard in South-east Asia to companies in Europe
or the United States. That was a mistake. The big companies are all
there, and all need local resources which are hard to find. More
co-ordinated 'world-wide' selling would have had a 'phenomenal'
result, Goodenough claims.

In this modest story old lessons may be restated. We'd gathered
quite a lot of knowledge of the Far East before we opened our office
there. Several of our people had good experience of working in the
area. Thanks to the Unilever connection, we met local companies and
learnt their needs and ways. That work expanded to other firms in
other countries. Head of the office was a man we trusted wholly and
who saw himself as part of our team. We blended the subtleties of
local knowledge with the resources of our main office. Increasingly,
we had a strong story to tell.

How different our Singapore development was from buying into a
region almost blind, with people you hardly know, whose loyalties
can easily lie elsewhere.

To Japan

Still, Singapore is Singapore. Japan, the giant, is something else. It seemed a wonderland, far too big and dazzling for us. I'd been there once or twice. The first time was to visit the World's Fair in Osaka in 1970. In Tokyo, my first call was at the British Embassy, a cluster of elegant buildings within their own compound. Sir Hugh Cortazzi was the commercial counsellor (later ambassador). He introduced me to Prince William of Gloucester, then a second counsellor, who was killed tragically soon after in a private plane crash. The prince looked at me. 'Going to Osaka, eh? Got a press pass?' I hadn't. 'Ah, then it's impossible. Outside every pavilion there's a two-hour queue. But wait . . .' He took me along a corridor to see the press attaché. The attaché rummaged in his desk until he found a thick, rich piece of paper, with the royal cipher deeply embossed in gold. He called his secretary and dictated something to her. In a moment she returned with the letter typed on the magnificent paper. 'No, it still won't do,' the press attaché said. Again, he pulled open one drawer of his desk after another, looking for rubber stamps. He banged maybe four or five roundels on the paper, then handed it to me. 'Here,' he said, 'try that.'

At the World's Fair press office in Osaka, after much peering, it was approved. I was given a press pass. It made all the difference. I strode into one pavilion after another – and I did write an article which appeared in *The Director*. So there may have been some justification for it all.

If ever there was a portent of things to come, it was the World's Fair in Osaka. Suddenly, the might and scale and efficiency of Japan was revealed.

Attachés at the embassy, both then and on later occasions, arranged for me to give presentations to senior managers of some of the largest corporations in Japan. I'd find myself in a room full of executives all dressed alike – dark-suited, white-shirted, grey-tied. After bowing and exchanging cards (printed in Japanese, a courtesy service of British Airways or BOAC as it was), we'd go to a conference room. They'd sit around a long table, I'd be at the end with a projector and slides. One catch was that you didn't know who the boss was. He never sat in the obvious place. You had to search him out. But how? It reminded me of a fearful moment in the army years before when, after three days of tests to see whether I was fit for officer training, I was told to march into a room and halt before a sergeant at a small desk. I gave my name. 'Turn right,' he ordered. I was startled to see I was now in a large room, with eight or ten officers seated at a long, polished table. I had to give my name again, but to whom? Then, too, the senior officer was not in the middle. Standing sharply to attention, eyes straight ahead, I had to find him. But at least they all had badges of rank on their epaulettes. These Tokyo groups were harder.

Who is the boss?

Facing these impassive executives in Japan what was I to say? Anything seemed an impertinence. My proposition, created in a moment of panic was refined with practice into this: Japanese companies had concentrated with wonderful success on the United States. Sooner or later they'd turn to Europe. But Europe is not as homogeneous. It is not one market, but several (that's true in the United States too, but I didn't know it then). Belgium is not like France. Italy is unlike Spain, the Netherlands unlike Germany. To sell well, Japanese companies would need to adapt their products and presentations to suit the various laws, tastes and preferences of each country. Being in London, I argued, having extensive experience in most of these countries, we were well placed to act for them. That was the drift. The cases I showed seemed to support the story.

The only fruit of these talks was that more than one company asked if they could put their designers in our offices. I was unwilling then, thinking that would help them develop in Europe without using us. Today, understanding their approach more, I would welcome their people, for from this first step a partnership would grow.

Here are some smaller points about doing business in Japan.

I once gave a talk to some 600 Japanese businessmen. Straight-forward enough, you may say . . . except that every sentence I uttered had to be translated into Japanese. My forty-minute talk took over two hours, a tedious endurance test for all concerned. So, if you are asked to speak in Japan, determine whether there will be simultane-ous translation. If not, cut your talk in half.

Without exception, the people you meet in Japan are charming and courteous. They gather to listen. When Shiseido, the cosmetics firm, asked me to talk to its design department, I found it was easier to perch on the edge of a desk and chat informally.

Simpler things, however, like being on time, can be a big problem. The traffic is horrifying. I went to see Dentsu, then thought to be the largest advertising agency in the world. I'd allowed plenty of time but, stuck helplessly in traffic, I arrived over an hour late. Housed in its own skyscraper, the marbled lobby had banks of lifts on either side, each manned by a girl trimly dressed in a crimson blazer, white pleated skirt and wearing gloves. They summoned the lifts, waved you towards one, then bowed as the doors slid together. I was shown to a room full of people who had been waiting. With embarrassed apologies I quickly put my drum of slides on a projector they had provided. The projector was a new model. My slides wouldn't eject. As I showed each slide I had to retrieve it with a comb, borrowed from one of the audience. It was not a good way to impress an audience. In short, always double the time you allow to get anywhere – and take your own projector.

Lateness is not unusual. I was fortunate to take part in a study tour organized by the Design Council and PA Consulting Group to see how Japanese companies develop new products. We travelled by bus to various parts of the country and frequently arrived one or even two hours late.

Apart from this shortcoming, the trip was spendidly arranged. Anyone who doubts the powers of Japanese business needs to go on such a trip. We were welcomed inside Sony and Sharp, Seiko and Minolta, Nissan and other companies. Every day we were in the next century. Glass doors slid open on verbal command. I even made a television picture zoom to a close up by telling it to, touching nothing.

For all its hazards, in my view, it is imperative for British and other European business executives to have strong working links with their opposite numbers in Japan. Sensing that, perhaps, even on my first visit to Japan I asked about design offices. The biggest and best office, I was told, was run by Kenji Ekuan. He is well known in Western design circles for the active part he played in ICSID (the International Council of Societies of Industrial Design). I went to see him.

Visiting his offices was a new experience. They were in a timber building in residential suburbs. I had to slip off outdoor shoes, put on slippers, bow a lot – it made me diffident, uncertain. But Kenji was accustomed to the West and gently we came to know each other.

His company designed products. That was ideal for us. What we needed, I thought, was some way of forging a link which gave us three things. First, some understanding of Japanese ways and Japanese business. This would take years, so the sooner we started the better. Second, access to new information from Japan. Third, introductions to Japanese companies who would need design in Europe.

Ekuan had the same interest in Europe. We agreed to co-operate. No doubt there was some formula for any financial benefit we might gain, but that was not the main motive for either of us. Kenji appointed someone to liaise with us and we chose a man to deal with his office. We imagined swapping designers too.

In London, some months later, John Beadle, my partner came to my room. 'You know we made that arrangement with the Japanese?' he said. 'We sent them all that stuff. But nothing is going on – shouldn't you get in touch with them?'

No more than four minutes later the phone rang. 'Harro,' a voice said. 'This is Kenji. Am in London, can we meet?' I hurtled to John's room. Then, struggling to hide my puffing, I strolled in. 'You wanted me to get hold of Ekuan,' I said, and added, as casually as I could, 'Well, he's coming in at ten tomorrow morning.' John was dumbfounded.

It had been a day of remarkable coincidence. At lunch I had met Martin Stevens and Walter Margulies, whose company, Lippincott & Margulies, was operating in London. We were standing at the bar of the Garrick. 'Tell Walter', said Martin, 'why you couldn't possibly have a company in this country with the initials SS.' 'Oh, no,' I replied, the Nazis still fresh in all our minds, 'it's out of the question.' At that instant I looked out of the window to see a huge truck going by painted from roof to springs with the initials SS. Then I'd rushed back from lunch to see someone from Chicago I'd never met. As one does, we swapped names. The only person I knew in Chicago was a man we'd worked with three years before and not seen since. No sooner had I said his name than the phone went. It was him.

When Kenji Ekuan came the next day we had a good meeting, but I was simply unable to entertain him that evening. After his great hospitality in Tokyo, it was possible he was affronted.

In such slight ways are relationships with Japan built or not. A month or two ago I went to an Anglo-Japanese dinner, also at the Garrick. It didn't occur to me to take visiting cards. (When young I was told one should never take business cards to dinner, but that wasn't the reason – I just hadn't thought.) The Japanese handed out their cards. Some English guests did too. Those that didn't committed a breach of etiquette.

I mentioned this detail because I believe courtesies are extremely important to the Japanese people. Nor should their good manners fool us into underrating cultural and social differences. Kenneth Grange, a British designer, went into a Japanese department store to buy a kimono. As he tried one on he noticed the petite shop assistants giggling behind their hands. Why? Kenneth, over six feet tall, and well-built, had been trying on a ladies' nightie.

Trying on a ladies' nightie

On to Australia

In Hong Kong once I ran into Sir Misha Black, a great friend and pioneer of design in Britain: with Milner Gray he started perhaps the first design office in London, in 1930. 'I was coming out here,' he told me, 'so I thought I'd just pop down to Australia.' He'd just returned. Tired out, he'd learnt that getting there is more than just a pop.

I was on my way to Australia to meet the chairman of Aspro-Nicholas, for whom we worked in England. It wasn't generally known that it is an Australian firm. The founders had come from Melbourne to England in the 1920s. They started by selling Aspro, advertising hard, then they fanned out into a range of other consumer products – Radox amongst others. We were hired to develop a world-wide corporate identity for them. The job took us to all their offices in Europe and the United States, and finally to their home.

Heeding Sir Misha Black's experience, I checked into the hotel in Melbourne on Saturday, for a meeting on Monday. At the desk the company had kindly left me a large box of their products, together with a bottle of whisky. They had also ordered a bunch of flowers – or rather a basket of flowers, the sort stage-door johnnies gave Marlene Dietrich. With an arching handle, maybe three feet high, it overflowed with blossoms. A 'buttons' – a boy wearing a pill-box hat and tight green monkey-jacket – carried it before him to my room.

An under-manager must have been on duty. 'Must be someone,' he concluded. 'Better be safe.' Within a minute or two there was a tap at my door. Would I accept these, the porter asked, with the manager's compliments? He brought into the room another basket of flowers, another bottle of whisky and a great bowl of fruit. A happy case of mistaken identity.

A wonderful country, Australia is full of surprises. At lunch in the boardroom of Aspro-Nicholas they served wine. 'Mmmm,' I said, 'this is superb. Do you export it?' 'No bloody fear,' was the taciturn reply.

Each evening the president and his wife invited me to dinner or took me out. It was time I repaid their hospitality. I asked a secretary the name of the best restaurant in Melbourne, then booked a table. When the president's wife heard where we were going she was pleased. Good so far. As we opened the door of the restaurant the *maître d'hôtel* beamed. 'Mr Peeldeesh,' he said, ''ow nice to see you.' We were old friends: he had come to Australia three weeks before from L'Etoile, in Charlotte Street, where I often ate. He led us to the best table. When a waiter brought menus (the size of posters) he tore them away.'You don't need them. I tell you what to eat.' Same with the wine list. If the president's wife wasn't impressed, she should have been – I certainly was.

The Nicholas job had several dimensions. First their products in every country had a different look: you'd hardly know they were made by the same company. Second was a more important point. The company had grown on the back of Aspro, but had developed into a multi-product group. In our opinion, they placed too much emphasis on that original part of the business. For one thing, people who worked on Aspro saw themselves as the first eleven; people working on other brands did not. That was bad for internal relations, if nothing else. Third, while they wanted a universal identity, we thought it important that the brands should be the 'heroes'. They could and should differ from each other. Finally, and my main reason for going to Australia, the chairman wanted to move out of OTC (over-the-counter) products – known less kindly as patent medicines – and into 'ethical' products – sophisticated drugs sold on prescription.

The company produced some already, but now wanted to concentrate on them. As so often happens, personal vanities may have been involved. The chairman perhaps sought the esteem that comes from having a serious scientific foundation bearing his name. To support his ambition, he pointed to his company's investment in research and development, then running at 2 million Australian dollars a year.

At that time we were also working for Hoechst in Germany. Their investment in pharmaceutical research was at least two hundred times as great. I argued that Aspro-Nicholas could only beat Hoechst, or similar giants, by luck. They were no match. Instead the company should do what it did best: packaged-goods marketing. In the event, they agreed. The company sacked most of its scientists in England, moved some to Melbourne and concentrated on developing more branded goods. In the next few years under the president's direction, the company leapt forward.

Australia is a fine country, but as a market, it assumes a low priority for many service companies. Not only is it a long way, still, but the cities are far from each other. In Perth one day I was talking to a civil servant about the need for 'import substitution, – to create one's own products instead of importing them. He agreed. After a while I realized what he meant by 'imports' were products coming from Sydney, in another state.

In time our connections in South-east Asia grew. While we worked directly and locally for companies in a number of countries, people came to us in London from Hong Kong, Colombo, Jakarta and elsewhere to ask us to design products or other things for them. Our people in London and Coventry (where we had a micro-electronics company) sought sub-contractors and suppliers in the Far East. As we felt more at home there and our experience grew, so did our confidence. The 'golden tomorrow' we had dreamt of was arriving. South-east Asia, or the Pacific basin, daily assumes more power, more importance. Links there are invaluable. Companies without them work with one hand behind their back.

11 International Spin-offs: Other Countries

A third of the fur sold in the world passed through one or other of three auction houses in a little cobbled street called Garlick Hill, near the Mansion House in the City of London. But one of them had a worry. For years mink breeders had sent their pelts to London for auction. Then, in the seventies, the Scandinavian countries set up their own auction houses, to keep the trade at home. We were asked to write and design a brochure to persuade breeders they were better off selling in London. (They were: London auctions were held more often, they attracted more buyers and they paid quicker.)

Although many of the British companies we worked for export their products and large groups span the globe, we were slow to realize what this meant. Our minds were too pigeon-holed. The bulk of our business was in Britain, but we wanted to be international, so we pushed out abroad. We assumed the two were different. It took us a long time to take advantage of the fact that London is the centre of a great deal of international business. Like charity, business begins at home, even international business. So we started to tell our British clients – and prospects – of our experience abroad. Many were intrigued by our arguments.

First, business everywhere was becoming more international, and that affected British firms as much as any others. We said we were able to help them. If we could satisfy German firms selling in Germany, why couldn't we serve British companies that wanted to sell in Germany? Second, our international experience enriched our ability to serve British clients. If, for example, we had worked at a high level for banks in Belgium, France, Greece, Indonesia, the Netherlands, Germany and the US as well as the UK, we were likely to know some of the problems banks face. Third, having offices in several countries, we were well placed to provide the consistent service international companies need.

There is a fourth, if less obvious, point. Working in other countries, facing new challenges, stimulates people. The experience refreshes their views. For designers, no less than anyone else, that is likely to increase their job satisfaction and improve the quality of work they do. Then there is the extra responsibility they carry abroad, where they *are* the company. You can see how being international sharpens the competitive edge.

Our reputation spread. Both Shell and BP approached us when they were looking for new designers. Raymond Loewy, doyen of American designers, had resigned the BP account. Word had it that he had his eye on Shell. Both jobs, wholly international in character, were going. How, we wondered, should we tackle them?

The line we took was this: with Shell, you could be sure, Loewy would go in with all guns blazing. His office was the biggest in the world, at that time the most experienced. He worked for many global corporations. Loewy himself was famous, perhaps the only designer ever to appear on the cover of *Time* magazine. I'd met him once or twice. In New York he told me 'designing products gives you prestige; designing packaging makes you money', an absurd truth I heeded and endorse. The second time we met, in Paris, he left abruptly because he was late for lunch with Brigitte Bardot. When he died, his sketches for work he'd done on the first space mission were auctioned at Sotheby's.

We couldn't match Loewy's prestige. There was no point in fighting on the same ground, so when we were invited to Shell for a preliminary chat I turned up with no notes, not a slide in sight. My aim was to be seen as a receptive listener, more than Mr Loewy was likely to be. The attempt failed. Shell wanted a design company able to match their scale. They chose Loewy.

With BP we took the opposite tack. They had been used to big resources. We'd show we could provide them. We researched the company at length, weaving what we knew and thought into a dazzling audio-visual presentation. Count Sigvard Bernadotte, then heading our office in Sweden, came to the meeting. So did the man who ran our company in Belgium. The head of our German work was there, and others. We rehearsed our presentation to the minute and practised answers to questions we were likely to be asked. My word, it was polished.

Eight BP executives came to the office. Things went swimmingly. The questions we'd foreseen popped up, one after another. Even those we hadn't thought of were answered impressively. One was: 'Have you any experience behind the Iron Curtain?' Yes, the Belgian replied. The day before he had returned from Moscow, where he had designed and put in place a pavilion for the Belgian Government at an international exhibition. We were like batsmen who take all kinds of bowling and knock the ball at will, to any part of the field.

The ball that caught us out was this: 'What level of the firm do you like to deal with?' I smelt the danger but before I could reply Sigvard said, 'Oh, the top. We must deal at the top.'

That was that. One silly reply wiped out all the work we had done.

Why was it silly? In retrospect it is easy to see. For one thing, BP were fed up with Loewy's imperious behaviour. He dealt only with the very top, above the people we were talking to, for our guests were second- or third-tier managers. Senior enough for us, they did not see themselves as the top executives of BP.

That presentation was perhaps the most researched, rehearsed and thorough we ever gave, yet it failed, just as the informal approach I'd made to Shell had done.

While all these great corporations make London a wonderful centre for international business, so does the inflow of companies from other countries. Elf, the French oil company, employed us to convert some 500 petrol stations they had bought in Britain. A Dutch company used us to design a large wholesale warehouse they opened here. An American bank asked us to design their executive offices in London, and so on.

Other companies come to London to find design and other consultancy services.

One day a man rang from Lopex, the advertising agency. He explained he had an Italian client who wanted consultants to handle the design aspects of a merger between two firms, Perugina, who made chocolates, and Buitoni, the pasta people. We got their annual reports, talked to Italians in the food business, researched their markets, bought their products. (That part was easy; Soho was just down the road.) When the Italians came our boardroom looked like an Italian deli. Their goods were everywhere. On slides we had charts from their annual reports interwoven with other facts we had gathered, as well as examples of our abundant work in the food business. It was ideal.

As they left, the agency man winked like a Belisha beacon. 'You've got the job,' he whispered. A week went by. Two. I rang. 'I've been too embarrassed to call you,' said the agency man. 'Do you remember the shirt you were wearing?' No. 'It was striped.' (These were the 'swinging sixties'.) Yes, now I remembered: at home we called that shirt 'One of our deckchairs is missing'. So? 'The client thought that shirt showed signs of levity.' For that reason we didn't get the job. And they were Italians, too. But then, I reflected later, both men who came had been to Harvard. That was in the annual report, clear to read. They'd come back more buttoned down, white-shirted, than we sybaritic Europeans recognized.

These examples show I believe in research. It used to amaze me how often people would come to the office to sell us something – themselves, maybe, looking for a job – without knowing a thing about us. They hadn't done a minute's homework. Why should you buy from, or employ, anyone so unthinking?

My striped shirt showed 'signs of levity'

Our diligence proved itself when we were commissioned to create a coat of arms for one of the Trucial States in the Persian Gulf. Mark Woodhams, a senior designer with us, took a thorough briefing from Arabists in London. He then spent several days in the library of the School of Oriental Studies. Gradually he came to select devices charged with meaning. This one stood for strength, that for justice, and so on. Mark created a shield with symbols within it. To our lay eyes it looked good. Then he checked it again with the Arabists. 'Oh, no,' they said, 'the scimitar *must* point this way. If it points that way it means . . .' (Death? dishonour? Something wrong.) Hard though it was to work in a strange visual vocabulary, the coat of arms came together. Then Mark wanted to show it in use. He phoned Rolls-Royce. Not only did the ruler of the country have a Rolls-Royce, the company knew which one and had a photograph of it. Mark sketched the new flag on it. Thanks to such thoroughness, his presentation was greeted with acclaim.

The Arab example emphasizes two points. First, the need to

understand the unstated significance of shapes, symbols, colours and words in other cultures. Languages unknown to us – Farsi, Burmese, Malay – warn us. But, and this is the second point, the same hazard applies closer to home. When satellite TV was first spoken of I went to meet an expert to ask what it meant. He outlined some of the problems we would face. He took baby food as his example. Even within Europe, laws governing what you can say and show on a package vary considerably. To work well internationally you have to know.

The Arab job succeeded because the designer was unable to assume anything. He had to find out, had to research every inch of the way.

Although it was never a goal, quite a lot of work from the Gulf came our way. One project was to design the interiors for a cultural museum to be built in an Arab country. It covered five acres. All one Christmas I wrestled with the task. Then things I'd forgotten from university days started floating into my consciousness. Poring over maps I came to realize that all the artefacts of interest in that region came from a thousand miles north of the city concerned. In other words, there'd be little to show. In advertising they say, 'If you've got nothing to say, sing it.' So we created an audio-visual experience to make the most of very little.

An old friend of mine, Eric Morgan, gave a talk on 'international business' in Zurich. He was chairman of British–American Cosmetics, a diversification of BAT. They had bought Yardley, Germain Montheuil, Lentheric and perhaps other cosmetics houses. Because he was making such a dent on the market, he attracted a large audience. Eric started by chalking one word on the blackboard: *hubris*. He talked about that word for forty minutes, how pride can lead one astray in business. I've often met it – executives who take us to a room full of their packages from around the world. More than one has said how unrelated they look. Would we make them all alike? Others want everything done the same way, wherever they travel . . .

Even though 1992 will bring the countries of Europe together and the wider world is surely shrinking, it will be many years before our histories are obliterated. Respect for regional variations, sensitivity to local culture is more than polite; it is common sense.

Packaging makes the point well. Designs we did for Indonesia, say, and which dominated the local market, would never pass the buying committee of any European supermarket. As perceptions differ, so must the language to communicate them. Needs differ too, as we often found. In Egypt, Portugal and Algeria, for example.

Egypt

Lonrho called just before Christmas one year to ask us to look at the packaging used in the pharmaceutical industry in Cairo. This became a rare case of me exercising some sort of *droit de seigneur*. I'd never been to Egypt and wanted to go, even though I knew little about the technical side of packaging and less about the Egyptian pharmaceutical industry. (It reminds me of how a friend, Richard Haddon, as deputy advertising manager for BAT, spent his life hurtling between Omsk and Tomsk and the further parts of the world; whenever a more congenial trip came up, to Paris or New York or Nassau, his boss would share the load: 'I think I'll do this one, Richard,' he'd say.)

I said I'd need a technical consultant with me. That was agreed. James MacChesney was such a man. With Lonrho's representative, a former naval commander, we flew via Paris to Athens. There the plane broke down. With all the other passengers, we were driven through the night to a concrete box of a package-tour hotel. Everyone milled around the reception desk, struggling to get a room. After one glance the commander said, 'Follow me.' He led us to the darkened and closed bar. For an hour we chatted peacefully, helping ourselves to the hotel's whisky. When the hubbub around the desk died down, the commander strolled to the night porter and muttered something. Within moments a stretched limo arrived. It whispered through the night to another hotel. My room was among the largest and most luxurious I have ever been in. By daylight I saw the hotel stood on rocks above a glistening bay – a beautiful setting. Still, MacChesney and I left at once to visit the Acropolis. We arrived as the great orange sun was rising over Athens and we strolled around the Acropolis alone, a memorable experience.

It was with some trepidation that we visited the pharmaceutical factories in Cairo. We needn't have worried. Even I could have helped them and for James MacChesney it was easy. They bottled purified water in an open room, with birds fluttering in and out and a goat, as well as clusters of people, peeking through the door. I never saw so many people. They were everywhere. Busily, James and I worked out what equipment the factory needed to mechanize and eleminate all these hand-tasks. How wrong. The local problem was not mechanization but unemployment. It was cleverer to think how to use the resource they had in abundance: people. Design, I realized more clearly than before, is always relative and specific. The idea of design as creating perfect objects is only sometimes right. It would have been absurdly wrong in Egypt in that plant at that time.

Between days of listless work, while the commander sat in his hotel room waiting for a call to visit 'the minister', we rode camels, climbed pyramids, visited the dusty and dishevelled museum, watched belly-dancing in King Farouk's former summer palace in the desert. Early one morning I flew to Luxor, once Karnak, then crossed the Nile and bumped in a springless taxi across the sand to marvel at the tomb of Tutankhamun and the Valley of the Kings.

Portgual

In Portugal too we found perceived needs were different from any we were used to. When we went, one family, the de Mellos, owned huge chunks of the country. A third of the national airline, TAP, the many-craned shipyard in Lisbon harbour, CUF, the country's oil business, construction companies, and more besides, were all part of their empire. But they were unknown abroad. Large contracts brought into the country were not coming to them. The US Air Force was a prime example: they were establishing a large base in Portugal, and all the infrastructure to go with it.

We were employed to design a corporate identity. Tim Williams, then in our office, created designs the family liked. When we presented them, we tabled a plan for implementing them. 'An early step', I remember saying, 'is to present this new design to your employees. Tell them why you have decided to use it . . . win their enthusiasm and support.' The de Mellos brothers, both most charming, looked at me blankly. Why tell the employees? It was an alien and wasteful idea to them.

Coincidentally, the country was torn by revolution within a few months. Perhaps we had glimpsed a reason.

Algeria

Vietnam and Cuba were shrines of similar struggle to Siné, the famous French cartoonist. His voice growled with emotion when he spoke the place names, always visibly moved. Siné had helped the Algerians during their war with France. For his pains, he was unwanted in his own country. He was allowed to live there (his house outside Paris was called La Maison Close, the symbol on his letter-head a red light), though not to work there. Instead, the Government of Algeria rewarded him. He was a hero. They gave him generous fees to work for the local oil company.

Siné persuaded the Algerian oil company that to compete internationally it needed the same design quality and confidence that they saw in Shell or Exxon or any of their global competitors. He took Philippe Rasquinet and me to meet the board. Like everyone in the company, the directors wore Mao uniforms – a tan-coloured, high-necked tunic and trousers. They, too, had been rewarded by the state for their part as 'freedom fighters' in the war.

After a great deal of research, we proposed not only a design programme but, more importantly, a programme to train their staff. We would make audio-visual programmes, have their staff in our offices and so forth. It was a large, sophisticated, two-year programme.

As we were leaving one day the man who ran their small design department took me aside. 'Next time you come,' he whispered, 'could you smuggle in some glue? Oh,' he added, 'and rulers.' They had neither. It is impossible to run a design office without glue. Their needs, in other words, were humbler than our grand scheme recognized.

Yugoslavia

As our international work became known letters arrived from the strangest places. Some I'd never heard of. In our financial department was Fergie, not the duchess but a former Royal Navy chief petty officer. A true old salt, square-shouldered, hands smartly behind his back (always hiding a smoking cigarette), he'd been everywhere. 'Fergie,' I'd say, 'where's so-and-so?' His reply was unchanging. 'Bloody hole . . . I was up there once and . . .' Off he'd go into another yarn. Fergie's opinion wasn't limited to the furthest points of the globe either. I asked if he'd ever been to Stockholm. Stockholm, 'the Venice of the North', is a beautiful city. Not to Fergie. 'Bloody hole,' he started, 'I was there once when . . .'

Yugoslavia was no exception; it was beginning to concern us.

The head of our product design group at the time was Roger Ford, an extremely able man. He had been getting on famously with the Yugoslavian equivalent of GEC, the state electrical company. Roger had seen an ad of theirs and written to them. He'd been to see them several times, received them in London, even mounted an exhibition for them. Suddenly, on the brink of a large contract, all went quiet. Roger couldn't understand it.

We asked Sir Peter Tennant, then with the British National Export Council, to advise us. 'You want to get on to Fitzroy,' he opened with. That was Sir Fitzroy Maclean, who had been sent by Churchill to decide whether Britain should support the Tito or the Mikhailovitch partisans. 'Then try Bobo [or some such name]', Sir Peter continued. 'She parachuted in too – with a broken leg.' It sounded like big talk to me, but next morning a bright English voice from the Foreign Office rang us. 'I understand you want to know about – [she named the firm]. How can I help?' That afternoon I received both an official telegram from the ambassador and a message from Sir Peter giving the gist of a private, fuller, message he had received from Yugoslavia. The company had trouble in the boardroom, it seemed.

Bobo dropped in too – with a broken leg

There may have been money worries too. So that was that. But consider how much time and effort those expert opinions had saved us.

I went to Yugoslavia twice, to give the same talk. The first time I flew to Belgrade and arrived late at night. Apart from a cleaner or two, there was no one at the airport, much less a bus or taxi. I made my way from the terminal to the main road. After a while, a car's headlights flickered into view. I waved the car to stop. In halting German I hitched a lift into town. At the hotel I wasn't expected. 'But there's a conference here tomorrow,' I said to the receptionist. He shook his head. Generally you know some other speakers or delegates, so I looked in the hotel register. There was no name I knew.

Puzzled, I ate in the hotel dining-room. A lady joined me. She said something I didn't follow, then '*Sprechen sie Deutsch?*' '*Nur ein bisschen,*' I replied. '*Parlate Italiano?*' she tried, taking another tack. '*Un poco.*' Her repertoire exhausted, she sighed and said, 'Fifty dollar?'

Next morning I found I had arrived three months early. The person in Belgrade who had translated the letter of invitation into English had used the wrong name for the month!

Equally disastrously, I returned three months later to give the same talk. Over Split the aircraft lurched in an electrical storm. Coffee I was drinking flew over my suit. Next morning I wore jeans, then unacceptable. The audience spoke no English, nor was there a translator. It didn't matter: through a paper-thin dividing wall, a rock band was rehearsing for an international contest. None of us could hear anything else. That was the only time I have gone straight to an airport and demanded a ticket for the first plane anywhere.

Confidential

There was a lot of travel. Several of us were abroad on any single day, working both for companies in other countries and for British firms. A project for British–American Tobacco taught us early the need for confidentiality, a good lesson to learn young.

BAT had the idea of marketing a new cigarette in Australia. It was to arrive on the maiden voyage of the Canberra, a great new liner. We were briefed, did the design and artwork. All was accepted. Advertising was prepared, everything was ready for the launch. Then the vice-chairman, Fritz Bodda, called us all together. 'It's all off,' he announced. Why? Because a competitor had pre-empted the name of our brand. It was simple: they had learnt the secret, mocked-up a package and photographed themselves buying it from a store. That was enough to destroy months of work. But how, I wondered, could anyone have found out BAT were developing this brand when everything had been done in secrecy? Had we been indiscreet? 'Oh, no,' said Bodda. 'Our competitors almost certainly have half a dozen people working here.'

Still, from that day on we were thrice careful. I like to believe that in all the years, with all the clients and all the staff involved, we never let slip a confidence. That, we all appreciated, was part of our stock-in-trade.

Fritz Bodda was a bear of a man. One day I presented some new designs to him, exquisitely drawn in fine detail by our skilled studio. Bodda reached in his desk draw and pulled out a box of coloured pencils. To my horror, he started to cover the design with alterations. I protested. Impishly, he looked at me and smiled. 'When *you* are vice-chairman of a company this size, then you too can have a box of coloured crayons.'

12 How to Sell Abroad

*So far we have watched the progress of one London-based com-
pany, offering mainly design services, as it built an international
business. The progress was not as smooth as Cleopatra's barge
gliding down the Nile, but more like that of a mountaineer who
inches forward with pain, scrambles across scree, strides across
surprising plateaux.*

*The next section of this book examines the steps, one at a time.
I cannot say what is the right route for you, though I do suggest
that some of the ideas that follow can make your map easier to
read: I hope they will help people who want to work internationally.*

*One suggestion: if you come across a suggestion that doesn't
seem right for you, take a moment to write your own, better or
more appropriate, idea.*

Although he ended up in Pentonville, the best salesman I ever met
was my boss in New York. He was irresistible, possessed of
charm, a silver tongue, quick wit, nerve and intuition. He used to
tell this story against himself.

At the end of the war he was in France trying to sell four fields
full of war-surplus equipment. He remembers trudging up wooden
stairs one rainy evening, perhaps in Dijon. At the end of a long
room in the dusk sat a man at a desk, lit by one green-shaded
lamp. My boss introduced himself, then talked about all the
material he had for sale: ball-bearings, Bren guns, bayonets,
barbed wire and the rest. The man put up his hand to stop him.
'Suppose,' he said, 'I could persuade His Holiness the Pope to issue
an edict to every priest in France to the effect that, after the
blessing, they should turn to the congregation and ask them to buy
your ball-bearings and barbed wire . . . Would you like that?'

'Why, yes,' said my boss.

'Even if I could do that,' said the Frenchman, 'I still wouldn't
buy your stuff.'

In other words, even the silkiest tongue won't sell the wrong goods. Think about the World's Fair in Osaka. The Russian pavilion soared over all others. At its pinnacle, visible from miles away, was the hammer and sickle. How, I wondered, would the Americans compete? I went to see. From the road, their pavilion was little more than a disappointing dome, hardly above ground level. Most of what they had to show was underground. Yet outside was a long queue. People stood for two, maybe three, hours to enter. Why? Because inside was the first chunk of rock brought from the moon.

Does that story confirm the view that if you have the right product you don't have to sell it? Does quality speak for itself? The question must be asked because many people still misunderstand marketing. They confuse it with selling, and they think it is not for them. It lowers their standards; to sell is 'un-professional'. At the first of her famous 10 Downing Street seminars on design, Margaret Thatcher spoke about marketing. Afterwards a distinguished designer said to me, his nose quivering at the vulgarity of it all, 'I was not brought up to sell.' In that phrase he expressed an attitude common among professional people, which has long outlived its time

Recently I saw presentations by the six architects competing for the job of building Terminal Five at Heathrow, a contract worth more than £1 billion. The day was extremely informative, although by default. Each firm, it was estimated, had spent up to £100,000 on sketch plans, drawings, even models. Yet none, in my view, sold well. Why? Someone explained to me that architects have a strict code of professional conduct: they may show no more than their work, 'So we never learn how to sell.'

The Design Council in London once rebuked me on the same lines. Selling, they told me, is unprofessional. Should that attitude linger, it won't last long. Every pressure is against it.

The truth is that without buyers and sellers there can be no companies, no jobs, no prosperity. What's more, selling is difficult, it takes all the professional competence you can muster. Whatever the vision, however clear one's strategy or excellent one's work, business comes from selling things. You can do this passively, by waiting for something to turn up, or actively, by going after work. The latter is the only safe way, the only way to be sure you go where you want and not where chance takes you.

The good news is that marketing and selling (two different concepts) can be taught. You can get better at both.

Hard start

'The trouble with first-time entrepreneurs', said Don Valentine, the man who funded Apple, 'is that they don't know what they don't know.' Selling is not so different. My own start was crowded with failure. As a magazine editor in Canada I had seen how preferment in my firm went to others, not least to people who brought in business. I decided selling is a skill to acquire. So I joined a design firm, both to help with their PR and to sell their services. I soon got the sack, not because I was lazy but because I didn't deliver results. I couldn't sell. I got another job, and the same thing happened.

One prospect I saw regularly was the Canadian company of ICI. Every few weeks I went to have a cup of coffee with someone there, always telling him what my firm did. One day, desperate, I asked him to give us a job. 'Of course,' he replied. 'I've been going to for months – I was just waiting for you to ask.' Now there was a lesson. For one thing, you don't get business just by describing what you do. For another, if you want a job, ask for it.

Starting is not easy. On the wall of one Montreal firm was a sign which read: YOUR VISIT IS THE CLIMAX TO AN ALREADY DULL DAY. Not many firms are like that, but some are. To the stress of trying to see uninterested people, persevering to persuade them, then seeing the work is well done, add the strangeness of other languages and customs and you see that selling internationally is not for novices. If, as a professional person, you think you shouldn't quite be doing it anyway, then getting business abroad really is tough.

In one of his books Negley Farson, the distinguished traveller and reporter, described how, for a year or two, he sold cars in Pittsburgh. With a partner, he won the largest order going. He told of the joy they felt on the way home. It was nothing to do with the money they'd earn – a point many people misunderstand – it was the fun of the chase, the thrill of the catch.

Imagine the satisfaction when months of work come together: when the board of the biggest chemical group in Germany appoints you, when the top executives of a great corporation in New York say 'yes', when Swedish machine-tool manufacturers and French perfumiers ask you to work for them. It's a thrill everyone in the company shares.

Peter Cree, who ran our company for a number of years, is emphatic: 'You must always sell, it keeps you looking out, to your customers, to see what they want. It helps you control the direction of your business, and it is wonderful training. Never', says Peter, 'stop being hungry.'

YOUR VISIT
IS THE
CLIMAX
To AN
ALREADY
DULL DAY

Reception room in a Canadian company

The marketing approach

Several cases in this book have shown that seven or eight discrete skills are needed to sell internationally. Part of the process is systematic, another part subtle and sensitive, a third vigorous and demanding. I will go through the steps one by one.

The starting point must be strategic, to decide what kind of company you want, who you want to buy from you, and where they are.

At first, I dare say, my firm sought work from anywhere we could think of. But in time our approach became more purposeful. We formed a clear idea of the place we wanted in Europe some years ahead. Then, with all the usual fits and starts, we made our way there. We started small, with limited risk, then became bolder. We took pains to work out which industries would grow in the future. We chose a few to focus on.

Our whole behaviour turned on these market-focused strategies. Quickly they overlapped and fed each other. The more we specialized

on a few industries, the better we were able to approach companies in those industries in other countries.

Theodore Levitt, when professor of marketing at Harvard, used to say, 'If you're not thinking segments, you're not thinking.' Our selling became more and more targeted. In early days, one of our people sent the same letter to 100 firms. He achieved nothing. When someone else wrote to six companies in one industry it led to four interviews and two jobs. But even that is probably too general. With experience, we stopped blasting the market with a scatter-gun. We shot with a rifle, identifying not just the industry and the company, but also the people in it and their possible needs.

While being open to opportunity, the aim must be a move from offering general skills to offering highly focused and informed skills, addressing the client's particular, identified, needs.

You can't do this without information. Most companies, dare one say, would do well to strengthen their information-gathering. When we started our information centre, people in the company were sceptical. I was always pressing them to use it. Later, they wouldn't move without the department's help. Of course, we would all say we study our customers. The difference, you learn from the more successful companies, lies in the intensity, the thoroughness with which it is done.

How do you choose which industries to concentrate on? Your present client list is a first guide. People often list this alphabetically, a tidy but unhelpful way. If you break your list of clients into industries you will see where you are strongest. I recall the managing director of Shell once advising people to 'do what they are good at'. His company's biggest mistakes, he said, had come from venturing into fields it didn't understand.

This focus can give you a competitive advantage. Take two design firms I know. One has worked for six financial institutions, the other for twenty-six. The first company, now targeting its marketing on the financial world, is building information about it and has sales material specific to it. The second company has not segmented in this way. To the banker, it will seem a generalist. My bet is that the first company will win more work in that field because it has focused on it.

From your general awareness, from newspapers, government figures, industry statistics and forecasting specialists, it is possible to see where growth is likely to be. The important addition is to look beyond one's own profession. Changes in technology, in education, in leisure and other aspects of life can give clues. By screening your guesses about the future through the sieve of your own strengths, it is often possible to arrive at a first list of industries to focus on.

Competitors

That list will be little use, however, if your competitors are stronger in those fields. Until recently, books on marketing talked endlessly about concentrating on the customer. Often they stopped there. Too soon. It is, after all, our competitors we have to beat. They may set the standards of performance, so knowing about them makes sense. I confess we never did this well. Although we kept files on our competitors, we rarely looked at them. That was a shortcoming.

The more we know about our competitors the better, and it is twice as true internationally. Before plunging, or even dipping one's toe, into another country it is sensible to have a sound idea of who you will be up against. What do they do? How good are they? Where are they strong and not so strong? The question to address always is simply put: why should clients choose you? What have you got that will persuade them to go to the inconvenience of dealing with people from abroad? Of course, in time, when you have something to show, being international gives you an edge. Initially, when you haven't, it is a disadvantage to overcome.

From this picture – of your markets, your strengths and your competitors – you have to carve out a definition of yourself which is different from, and more appropriate than, that of your competitors. It is not enough to be good. You have to be better in the dimension which serves the customer or client best. That sentence embodies the need for all kinds of information.

Perhaps any company has to behave like a chameleon, adapting easily to suit its environment, its clients and its opportunities. You have to be both constant and light on your feet, an apparent contradiction.

If it is to prosper, a company must match the hopes, needs and preferences of its potential clients – and do it more precisely than its rivals. How tricky that can be, when every client is unique. Companies need to turn themselves inside out. What usually happens is that people enjoy certain kinds of work, they develop their skills, then look around for someone to buy them. A better way is to look around first, to see what is needed, where the gaps are, then shape one's company to fill them.

What we found, too, is that if you offer more than one service, you may have to sell them differently. That is plain when the businesses are obviously unlike each other. In our case, we had several market-research companies, two micro-electronic firms, and a company which sold sophisticated financial services, as well as our design business. Of course, each sold in its own way. But even within one firm, the main design company, we found the need to differentiate. We had five 'practice areas', as we called them: corporate identity, product design, new product development, packaging, and space (mostly retail) planning and design. It took us time to see they were different businesses being sold to different people. Having one set of standards for them all, as we did for years, was foolish. As they developed, each part of the firm had its own fee scales, time scales and ways of selling. They sold to different people with different offers.

It is worth listing the competitive strengths and weaknesses of each part of your company, then developing promotional matter and sales arguments to match. In the end, except for our published annual report, my firm didn't have a general brochure, so committed were we to this idea of specialization.

It goes back to the word 'hubris'. We may be pleased as Punch turning the pages of a glossy brochure which displays all the work we've done, across a range of industries, but, on the whole, potential clients are interested in their own problem in their own business. Indeed, showing your range of work can position you as a generalist, rather than a specialist. This makes you vulnerable to the competition of any other generalist, and unarmed before any specialist whom the client believes understands his or her particular concerns. The general rule must be to talk to clients about *their* problems and to show your experience in *their* field.

While I would always advocate this specialist approach, there are dangers to it. We conducted research among our clients from time to time, to find what they knew and thought about us, the quality of our work, our service and so on. It was a shock to learn that clients using one service often didn't know of others we provided. Yet how hard it is to be firm. I went to see the marketing director of United Biscuits. Following my belief, I showed him one example after another of biscuit packages we had designed. At the end, showing off, I zipped through slides of other work we had done. He stopped me when he saw a shop we had designed in Sweden, for Georg Jensen. That interested him. Maybe his company was thinking of going into retailing, or buying a company in Sweden. I don't know. And that is the point: you often don't know what is in the client's mind.

The moral seems to be to put your goods in the window.

There is another point, one to encourage smaller firms. At home we know, or have a sense of, which companies are the largest, most reliable, most thorough or the best. Although such impressions may be false, they go before a firm, smoothing its path. Once abroad, the game changes. The competitive pecking order we live with at home may not exist in other countries. Suppose two Korean firms approach you. Would you have any preconceived idea about the merits of either? Probably not. This gives smaller companies the chance to compete on their merits more equally.

Smaller firms may feel they cannot compete abroad. With 1992 – and the years following it – about to change our lives for ever, that must be a worry. If they have nothing special to offer and are reluctant to make the necessary effort, they may be right – they will just be further away and more expensive than local suppliers. But if their smallness means they are more specialized, or their service is better ('we try harder'), then they have advantages. It comes back to knowing your market and understanding your competitors.

If the need for knowledge is the first lesson, and the need for 'segmentation' the second, then differentiation is the third. One key to that is innovation: either to provide services which are markedly better in some way or to create new services. This last way is best of all. It gives you freedom. Much of the work we built abroad came from services not available there. Offering new services, or being demonstrably better in some way, we created our own markets. Corporate-identity work was one example. Our methodology and experience had few equals. Our system for developing new products was another. Using fax to serve clients in the Far East was a third.

Everything one sees or hears about a business, including the demeanour and drive of its people, contributes to its marketing. Some people see marketing as a function, to go in a tidy box like every other discipline. I don't. Marketing is about deciding on aims and positioning a company to achieve them. Once you have a comprehensive strategy, it is about *doing*. Sooner or later, as Peter Drucker, one of the world's most profound business theorists, has said, 'everything degenerates to work'.

Who does the work?

Suppose you decide to sell in other countries. You've worked out where you want to go and what you want to offer. Who's going to do the hard part? In smaller firms this a worry. The boss should start, but he is busy. Who then? The answer is the boss. Only if he tries can he know the problems. Only by feeling the job at first hand will he know how difficult it is and what commitment is necessary. His promise to sustain effort for years is vital.

Perseverance is essential. You can't build international business by popping over to Milan or Paris for a few agreeable days. Nor can you do it sitting at your desk. There is no substitute for being in the country, meeting people, learning and becoming known.

You find heads of businesses who, once they have been involved in the strategy, leave its implementation to someone else. In time this may be necessary, but view the approach sceptically. For one thing, they'll never learn how much more difficult it is to do business abroad than at home, nor how the demands of customers or clients differ. They may hear it, but won't *know* it. As a result, they won't make proper allowances or provide enough support long enough. And, a mistake we've all made, they will expect results too soon. Most important of all, while the boss is at home international business will always remain subsidiary. That just won't work any more. All business is international from now on.

For all those reasons, even when international teams are in place, I'd want the boss to keep his hand in.

In our case, I led the way. So, in time, did the head of each practice area. Each boss sold and serviced. We tried hiring salesmen. With a couple of exceptions, that didn't work. We found the client, rightly, wants to deal with a specialist, someone who knows the business through and through. We tried hiring designers who could present well. The risk there is that you may turn down the really creative designer in favour of someone who looks good. Should one person enjoy both qualities, and we were fortunate to have a number who did, that's perfect.

In *The Marketing of Professional Services* Aubrey Wilson maintains 'You need a professional who can sell, not a professional salesman.' In the end we took the view that direct, face-to-face contact between the client and the person who is going to do the work (in our case, designers and others) is the right way. So it is. Then we backed them up with people who, today, would be called design managers. We evolved teams, one person to get the work, analyse the problem, establish the brief, plan the programme (with the designers, financial people and others), handle the admin, make dates and so forth. The other, the senior designer, would be responsible for creative quality. We fought against any kind of hierarchy. Some people were better at one thing, some at another. But if there was an argument, our natural position was to back the designer.

The important point, in my view, is to have as many people as possible engaged with the client. The idea of having people sitting at their boards or desks waiting to be fed by a salesman is anathema to me. The likely breakdown in responsibility, teamwork and communication is all too obvious. That way lies poorer performance and lower quality.

What about languages?

Do people who meet clients need other languages? Of course that is best. All staff should be encouraged to learn other languages. But the principle is this: clients buy professional knowledge; it is far more important to know your subject than to know another language. Having hired people whose main virtue was that they spoke French or German or Dutch, I am sure of this priority. Of course, in time we were fortunate to bring in specialists from the countries we were serving. That was ideal: they were specialists who spoke the language. Based in our offices, they learnt our ways and were backed up by secretaries and others from the countries concerned. Most of our correspondence, reporting, and billing was in the local language.

That brings us to another kind of preparation. Doing business abroad touches everyone in the firm: financial people will have to cope with exchange rates and letters from their opposite numbers in client companies, lawyers will have to translate your terms of working, secretaries will take calls from other countries, specialists in the office will have to work in other dimensions, use other terms. The culture of working internationally must be spread and worked at. When a Belgian client visited us he was greeted by a French-speaking receptionist. When Germans came a German secretary took their coats, gave them coffee, often attended meetings.

In practice, many of the business executives you meet in other countries speak excellent English but this is not always so. Why, one might ask, should it be? In practice, we may be less effective than we want to be if we assume everyone understands every word. You remember how, even in Sweden, we may have lost a client for that reason.

The hazards of language run both ways. We saw in France how I lost a good job when, speaking French, I got a decimal point wrong. But there can be nicer surprises. Presenting their designs to Priba, the Belgian retail chain, two of our people were saddened when the client kept saying *'terrible'*. They found out later that he meant 'wonderful'. Risky or not, it is certainly courteous (and common sense) to use the language of the country you are selling in.

How to find your customer

Committed and prepared, how do you find people to sell to? In Britain there are plenty of places to go for help (see Appendix). Trade associations and professional bodies have links abroad. Government departments are storehouses of information and British embassies, as we've seen, can be wonderfully constructive. There is a caveat: over years, I suspect, they have built a defence mechanism to brush off the casual enquirer. Prove you are serious, however, and they'll help enormously.

Yet there is an even easier way to start. Analyse any service business and you will find that a company gets a great deal of its work from people it knows or from referrals or repeat business. However diligently we sold, and despite all our good systems, time and again work came from friends met at parties, over the dinner table or at conferences. Maybe it shouldn't be so, but it is – we all prefer to do business with people we know.

That also applies to your existing clients. Your credentials are established with them, they are comfortable using you. What we did for years was to separate in our minds existing clients from new ones we were after. Our selling was outwards, to new firms, new territories. We didn't neglect the firms we worked for, but neither did we look to them for more work. It took us a long time to realize that our existing clients were our best prospects. Once that was understood, we mined away ('burrowed' was the term Peter Cree used) in our client companies. We always tried to fan out from our starting point to more and more divisions within the company.

When we told clients of our international experience they were often glad to use us in other countries. That worked in a number of dimensions. A large Dutch dairy co-operative retained us to help sell their products in Africa, South America, the Gulf and developing countries. If clients are happy with you they can give you work abroad or introduce you to their subsidiaries and friends in other countries. Their introduction more than takes the chill off any 'cold' sale you try to make.

What happens, too, is that people change jobs. We worked for one client first at Smiths Crisps, then he moved to Eire and took us there. Later he joined Arthur Baustedt, a German food company. Working for people on his staff, we redesigned all that German company's packaging. When he moved to another German firm he again took us with him. From Ericsson in Sweden we got work in Italy. A man we worked for at United Dairies moved to Nashar, a trading company in Saudi Arabia, and gave us work there.

We had many similar examples, but we took pains to stay in touch with clients. We told them, regularly, what the firm was doing.

Though life is full of surprises, it makes sense to go where potential clients are to be found. We visited trade and professional associations in countries we were interested in, offering to speak at conferences they organized, or write in their journals. Sometimes this worked more rapidly than we expected. I remember going to see the man in the state government of Connecticut responsible for building their exports. He met me off the train, then took me to his rambling, book-strewn, white-timbered house for coffee. There he took a phone call. 'It's all right,' he said, 'I've got someone who will do it.' He turned to me. The speaker at the lunch organized for that day had dropped out: would I mind taking his place?

You learn a lot from these trade associations, and if they ask you to speak, they provide some kind of endorsement. Better still they bring clients to you. There are people everywhere who need what you provide; you don't know where they are, nor do they know where to turn for help. Talks and articles sometimes help them find you.

PR

While that proved true, I never looked to public relations to bring in business. When it did, it was a bonus. Our idea was to put our thoughts, our experience and our name into people's minds. We were aiming at a climate of acceptance. To us, PR was part of our marketing, so we focused it on the industries which interested us. We didn't try to put our name everywhere, as many others in our field did. They liked to appear in *Design* magazine where they and their friends in the profession could admire it. Not much to be said for that, we thought. It smacks of introspection.

Once, in Canada, I was production editor of a movie magazine. (I chose and used, the first picture of Marilyn Monroe wearing a sack. The caption said she'd look beautiful in anything.) From those days I remembered one film star advising others in Hollywood, 'Never believe your own publicity – good advice which guided us.

When commercial television started in Britain I was working for a design office in London. 'We should watch that,' I said to one of the partners, 'it is sure to become very big.'

'Oh,' the partner replied, 'I never watch television. That is what ordinary people do.'

A week or two later, that partner suffered a slipped disc and went to a private clinic. I visited her. By her toes, at the foot of her bed, was the largest television set you have ever seen. It had been lent by a client. 'Television, eh?' I commented. 'Yes,' she replied, her aplomb and snobbery intact, 'it's rather amusing, one sees so many of one's friends.'

Being clear about your audience is very important. We'd often come across clients who made something – china, say – and we'd ask who they wanted to buy their goods. 'Anyone,' they'd say. 'Everyone is a potential customer.' With a few exceptions, this is untrue. Skilful companies identify their customer profile with care. Public relations and other forms of communication should be as refined.

Telling letters

If public relations is, by its nature, long-term, writing letters to prospective clients isn't. That's both here and now and an indispensable part of building business. Of course that is common knowledge and widely practised, but most letters I've seen are so dreadful they wouldn't shift ice-cream in the desert – or, to quote John Le Carré, 'sell hay to a rich horse to save his dying mother on her birthday'.

For a while I worked for an American direct-mail house called O. E. McIntyre. (McIntyre had spent his career with what was then the largest direct-mail firm in the world. When he retired at sixty-five he started his own company with his two sons. Within two or three years it was larger still.) McIntyre's company had shot ahead because it could prove it delivered twice the results of any other company. I asked him how. 'There are only two elements,' he replied, 'the quality of your mailing list and the quality of your letter.' I'd expand on this to list six elements:

1 The accuracy of your aim: find the right person.

2 Your message and its relevance to that person.

3 A demonstration or promise of benefits.

4 Your style.

5 A suggestion of action you will take in a few days.

6 The way you follow up.

Add two more: persistence and luck.

It takes research to find out who are the right people in the right companies for you, but it is easy to do. As I said, if your letter can start with an introduction from a friend of the prospect that is ideal.

What you often see is letters about 'us' and 'our'. 'You' and 'your' is better. The letter should hook the readers' interest at once with an idea you've had about their company, something you've learnt about it, some news of relevance to them, perhaps something you have done for a company in their field. Cite results whenever you can.

Your letter should propose action (you realize how busy they are, so you will call their secretary in three days to ask who they think you should talk to . . .). Leaving it to the recipient to contact you, as some letters do, seems to me limp. You are asking the client to shift the force of inertia in your favour. Offering alternatives can help too. ('Of course, I'll come whenever suits you, but I expect to be in Munich on 13 and 14 May, and wonder whether one of those dates . . .')

The follow-up phone call is crucial. The aim is to set a date for a meeting or to find the name of someone else to meet. Either way, you move forward.

Once identified, whether you meet them or not, all prospects should go on your mailing list. Mailing lists are your garden, to sow, weed and enjoy the fruits thereof. Someone in your firm should nourish them, constantly scanning journals and newspapers in the country you are interested in. Every few months strive to send news, a reprint of an article or something to people on the list. We've already noted how useful that can be.

It can take months, even years, to bring in a client, as we saw with LM Ericsson. Peter Cree estimated that we sold, one way and another, to them for twelve years, including following one key man from his previous firm before they commissioned us.

Precision is as essential as persistence. I once wrote to Sir George Harriman, then chairman of British Motor Holdings, which had brought together large chunks of the British motor industry – Austin, Morris, Rover, Jaguar, MG and many other marques. We'd been looking at the group and thought we saw ways to help it. My letter was three paragraphs long. Plainly, it struck a chord. By return we received a two-sentence letter asking us to see the company secretary. We did. Next morning there was a letter on my desk to say 'go ahead'. It led to a very large programme of work employing thirty-four people full-time.

Some letter, I thought. So I sent a similar one to the chairman of Vickers, which in our view was in need of much the same services. Next morning I took a call from Vickers' head of corporate affairs. In a rage, he threatened to take me to court for my impertinence. So there you are: what was precise in one case wasn't precise in another.

Of course, most letters don't work, certainly not quickly. But some do, and that is why they are indispensable. I think our statistics when we were experienced and thorough, showed that two and a half letters, followed up, led to one meeting. Two meetings led to one proposal. Most of those led to jobs in time.

Generally speaking, though, from tentative introductions it can take months of nursing and patient building to move a client towards commissioning you for the first time. Any suggestion that one can simply sweep in and swing busy executives in one swift strike would be misleading.

Is this steady effort worthwhile? Peter Cree once worked out that of the eight major corporate-identity programmes he was handling at one time (several global in scale), five came originally from cold sales.

Planning the meeting

Help! The person you have contacted says yes, he or she will see you. Time for more intense research. The more you know about that company, the more confident you will feel and the more pleased the prospective client will be. One step is to try to get others in the firm together at the same time – seeing several people helps a lot. But there are other preliminaries. Philippe Rasquinet and I were going to see the head of the Banque de Suez, in Paris, the climax of months of beavering through friends of friends and considerable research. Experienced by now, we were flying over the night before. Thick fog grounded all aircraft. Undeterred, we drove through the fog to Southampton, had a meal, then took an overnight ferry. At Le Havre, the fog was as bad. Philippe drove blindly at high speed to Paris. We arrived a moment before we were due, then walked in punctually. My trouble was I couldn't think of a word of French. I think I need to be in the country at least the night before just to hear the sound.

Another time in Paris, where I had arrived a night at least before an important meeting, I remember waking up to a brilliant morning. After a leisurely breakfast, I decided to stroll to the company I was to see. I arrived ten minutes early. Elegantly done, I thought, until I found the company had moved from the centre to Neuilly, half an hour away at least. It sounds silly to say 'make sure you've got the address right', but after that I've always confirmed it with the client.

The main preliminary, of course, is to plan your presentation. Even now I am amazed at how casually many people approach this. They pick up a folder, grab some flip charts or slap a drum of slides together and off they go. That is no way to convince a client that you care about them. The more you prepare a meeting the better is will be. As the Albert Heijn example (and many others) showed, we tried to visit our clients' outlets or offices, look at their products in shops, or talk to others in the same industry, before going to see anyone.

We used to hold little meetings among ourselves in the office, when one person would outline what he or she knew of the company, and others would suggest approaches that might interest it. Talking this through helps establish the objective of the client meeting, and that encourages you to tailor your presentation to meet it.

Presenting

My experience of presentations, including my own, is that they are too windy. We spend far too long loving the work we have done, showing one case after another, and nothing like enough time addressing the client's needs. It's the difference between a parade, where all the troops look splendid, and a battle, where they are marshalled to achieve an aim.

Before the meeting plan what you want to say and the most interesting way to say it. Rudi Beck used to distinguish between a logical sequence and what he called a 'dramaturgical' sequence. Another military axiom helps: parcel your facts into *must, should, could*. That is to say, list the facts you *must* get across, not being afraid of repetition. Decide the ideas you *should* convey. Then think which are less important and *could* be told if you have time. That helps one to focus. Plan how to get each part of your message across, bearing in mind the advantages of varying the means. Slides, yes, flip charts, yes, but something to touch, too. If more than one of you is to be present (and that's best) decide on a role for each to play. As we saw with Marsh & McLennan, it doesn't hurt to rehearse arguments and practice replies to questions you might expect.

People who are actually going to do the work, should any arise, should be at the meeting. It is one thing for prospective clients to meet the boss, persuasive as he may be, another for them to realize that the job would be done by others. And if those others are at the meeting, see they take part fully. Having juniors sitting there like bumps on a log, afraid to speak, does nothing to inspire confidence.

The next step is to prepare the room you are to present in. Secretaries will usually let you in early to do so. How many of us have tried to show slides in a room which can't be darkened? Or, having said hello to the client, found ourselves on our knees searching behind a desk for a socket – which takes the wrong size plug? Finding snags like that in advance is prudent.

For ITT we were to give a day-long presentation in Brussels. We arrived the night before to set up the room: projector focused, spare bulb handy, papers neatly placed on the table, even matches with our name by each ashtray. We looked around the long room. All perfect. We switched off the lights and left. Next morning, ready for the 8.30 start, we arrived to find the room stripped bare. ITT's sense of security was the cause.

In Copenhagen I relied on the host's projector. It didn't so much as break down as never start. I had to perform in mime, waving my arms as if I was conducting Verdi without an orchestra.

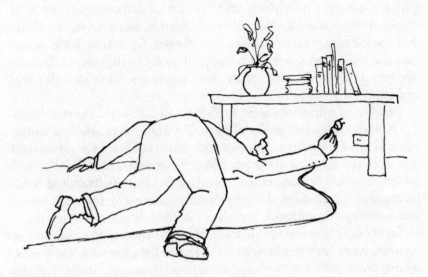

Looking for a socket in a client's office

As part of the Marsh & McLennan job our people presented to Bowrings in London. They used slides, shown by a 'rear view' projector operated by a technician behind the screen. The projector broke down so when Peter Cree wanted to change a slide he had to tap the person in front of him, who tapped another, who tapped the screen. 'What a lovely team you've got,' said Bowring afterwards.

Even today, in this electronic age, you can't be too careful. We still get it wrong, after years of experiencing every hazard there is. I went to present slides to a secretary of state. His staff had provided a screen but couldn't find a projector. Fortunately (experience telling) I'd taken one, but there was nowhere to put it. I had to cradle it in my arms, the pictures shaking and wobbling wildly with every move I made. Not ideal.

As to the meeting with the prospective client, there are so many variations, it is foolish to generalize. But I will describe one possible sequence so you can see how to improve it.

When you meet the client, and after the courtesies, tell the client who you are and how you intend to spend the next hour. Ask if he or she agrees.

Very briefly, explain what you do and who you have worked for in their field. Slides may help. At this early stage of the meeting interest is high. It is worth getting your main points across here as clearly and visually as you can. Always make sure your company's name is stated and remembered. We learnt this the hard way. In London once we gave a presentation to Mowlem, the construction company. Because it semed to go well, we were disappointed to learn a few days later that the job had gone to a competitor of ours. By chance, soon after, I met the chairman's wife at a cocktail party. 'Oh,' she exclaimed, 'we've just hired the most marvellous designers. They did [this job] and [that job].'

'But, but,' I burst out tactlessly, 'that's all our work. We did those.'

The lady called her husband over. He went ashen. He had simply phoned the wrong firm. That was our fault, not his. How often have you admired an ad without recalling the brand it sold? How much advertising sells a competitor's product because its branding is not memorable? Branding, that construction company taught me, isn't just for soap companies.

Try to get clients to speak about their problems, who they are up against, what they might need from you. Then, perhaps using slides again, show one or two case histories which are relevant to the company and their circumstances. In every case, state the case tersely: the problem, what you did, what the results were. Sell the benefits.

Then, with the projector off and the lights on, take time to describe how you work, your method, how you related to people in your other client companies. Use flip charts, flow charts. Show prospective clients what they may expect to get at each phase of the project. The aim of this slot is to assure the clients that you are methodical and reliable. Bring up the subject of money if you can. Often we are too shy to introduce it in the conversation. You should feel for guidelines, the sort of worries the clients have, or objections they might raise to using you.

Always take time to summarize. Peter Cree and I once went to a seminar on selling. It was delivered by two boisterous Americans; not entirely us, we thought. But one phrase stuck in the mind: 'buttonhole the benefits'. One undid his waistcoat, then did it up. 'Button-hole-the-ben-efits,' he repeated, a button at a time. That was good advice. As your presentation draws to a close remind the audience of your salient points, why they should use you. Neither Peter, nor I, nor others did so invariably, but when we left a meeting we'd kick ourselves if we had forgotten.

From the tenor of the meeting you can judge how far to go but, remembering my experience in Canada, it doesn't pay to be too shy. You need to come away from the meeting with something to do: a proposal to write, someone else in the firm to talk to, other branches to visit, or just a reprint or article you promised to send. If you have a quarter of a chance, get out your diary to look for a convenient date to see the prospect again. They will open theirs and you'll make a date.

Next day, of course, write to say thank you, and outline the next steps. The essence is to start building a dialogue, leading to a shared ambition to set up a project well, one that fits the client's needs and resources.

Some advantages of the framework described here are:

- You set the tone of the meeting.
- You look efficient and courteous because you are treating the client's time with respect.
- The client is pleased to see you have taken trouble to plan the time.
- The people you've met are at ease because you have told them what to expect.
- You keep the presentation lively by breaking it into parts.
- You get the client to talk. They see that you are a good listener, that you are worrying about their problem, and you show you have the understanding to help solve it.
- Having a strict time plan keeps you to the point. Seductive as they may be, you haven't time to go into the finer details of every job.
- You introduce the client to the people who will do the work. That is reassuring, too.
- By using more than one medium, you hold attention.
- You see the meeting as a targeted sale, rather than as a review of your past work.
- You address the client's problems rather than your enthusiasms.
- You focus on next steps. What can you do now to move you forward?

Having seen many presentations from numbers of companies, I am confident that the spirit of what is written here is constructive.

Overcome objections

The crux is to gear everything to the prospective client's needs as you perceive them. What do clients want? What are they afraid of? What would decide them to choose your company rather than another?

Sadly, it is simplistic to say that the quality of one's work is all that counts. If you are coming from another country, in some cases you may be thought to be better than local competitors (a myth, often devoid of foundation, which persists), but the insecurities to overcome may be more powerful.

Indeed, reassurance may be the key word for international selling. I have written a short list of some assurances one should weave in and out of every presentation. See if you agree.

Experience

Experience in the client's country may provide the greatest comfort. As was the case with Marsh & McLennan, people often say 'Yes, yes, you may be wonderful in England, but things are different here. What have you done in this country?' Breaking into a new market is very like getting your first job. You can't get a job until you've had experience, and you can't get experience until you have a job.

For newcomers to international business that is a hard one to overcome. This is one reason why work in other countries for your UK clients can be so helpful. With them you leap the gap.

Another way is to join forces with a local office. While it overcomes one objection, though, it may lead to complications, as you've seen from our experience. Though often a good solution, it is not one to be entered into lightly. Another way is to invite the client to visit your offices or suggest a small, safe project they can test you by. We also tried 'buying' an entry to a new market by charging less than usual, but that is risky too. Having started with one fee level, it isn't easy to lift it. Mark you, Japanese companies put market entry and market share above immediate profit; maybe it is right to do so.

Experience in the client's field provides comfort, too, especially if you have worked for rivals they admire. Still better, perhaps, is to show experience of the particular problem the client faces. NVWB, the Dutch road-builders' association said they chose us because their real concern was with their internal relations, an area of work we knew. 'The major criteria for our choice', they wrote later, 'was the emphasis you placed on the need for communication, diplomacy and persuasion to win support.'

Understanding

Understand their needs. They may be met by showing work for companies like theirs, particularly if they share the same problems. Cockerill in Belgium was a good example, You recall we concentrated not on our design quality, which we supposed any competitors would, but on the difficulty of effecting change in a large organization. Surely, that was his daily concern. We hadn't worked in the steel industry before, but had met his problem many times. That strategy, the decision to focus there, came after much thought.

Reliability

Most presentations I've seen dwell on the work the firm does, but take for granted or ignore aspects which might concern the clients a lot. How safe would they be with you? How would they defend themselves if things went wrong? It is worth describing your work method, to assure the clients you have the means to keep promises. Examples of satisfied clients may also be telling. Talking about the admin side of work may bore the presenter, but will interest the clients. Above all, they need to feel safe.

Cost Control

This is another basic worry. You need evidence to reassure the client that their financial commitment is safe with you. We described our hourly-rate methods, time sheets and strong financial back-up. We also showed letters from clients who had congratulated us for delivering what we had promised on time and on budget.

We sold large jobs a phase at a time. The end of each, we said, was a cut-off point: the client could stop the project then and be charged only for the work done thus far. That was another comfort, although I remember only two clients using it.

Service

People abroad will worry that because you come from far away (culturally and psychologically, if not geographically) your service will be less than they might expect from someone local. That, as has been said, is a critical objection to overcome.

The doubts and worries and uncertainties you have to overcome are sometimes expressed, often not. It is up to you to winkle them out and deal with them. True at home, it is several times truer when you venture into other countries. And, as Beverly Baxter, a Canadian journalist who became a British MP, used to say to young writers, 'Always state the obvious.' That applies here too: what is obvious to you may not be obvious to the client.

Your proposal

If you do well, the client may invite you to submit a proposal. 'Hoorah,' you might say, 'the selling is done.' We are inclined to see a written proposal, or estimate, or whatever you call it, as a formal, legal definition of what we've offered. We outline the project, describe the work plan, define the fees, state the legal understandings. That's not enough. There is a simple reason: it is most likely that your proposal will be read and judged by people who have neither met you nor seen your work. This means that the written proposal must be, though subtly expressed, a further selling effort. As well as confirming details you have discussed, it has to re-affirm your competence, character, experience and fitness for the job.

What we did often enough when a client had asked us to submit an estimate of fees and a work plan was to whoop our way down the street and into the first bistro for a celebratory drink. Days later, we'd send our careful proposal, all nicely typed. Then we waited keenly for confirmation to start work. Sometimes it came, sometimes it didn't. The initiative had passed from us to the client. Our prospect had to win support within the company.

With experience, we learnt how to hold more initiative longer and to reduce the risk of rejection. For example, having built a good rapport with the people we were dealing with, they were often as keen to go ahead as we were. Invariably, they would need the support or agreement of colleagues. So we used to ask them to advise us how to write the proposal to satisfy the others. What should the proposal contain? How should it be phrased? Who should we be sure to include in the work programme? Which locations should we visit? What would be the best way to handle the money questions? Their guidance made a fundamental difference to the quality and precision of our document.

We took great care over the introductory section where we outlined the problems and needs to be satisfied. Often this clarified the client's own thinking. 'It is astonishing what you've learnt about us in one hour,' clients would say, little realizing the patient work we had done both on our own and with our contact in the company.

Whenever we could we tried to present our proposal to the board or whoever decided, face-to-face. I have heard people say it is wasteful to make a special journey to another country for this purpose, but I disagree. What is particularly good is that not only do you add another brick to the wall of confidence, but you can hear and deal with objections on the spot.

Once we realized that the proposal was more than a formal offer, we included a section on project management, exactly who would report to whom for each phase of the work. We described the people in our team who would be involved, with a note of some of their experience. We showed a detailed work plan with a critical path, review dates and cut-off points. We mentioned other companies we had worked for, sometimes with brief case histories (for the executives who hadn't seen our presentation) and included nice letters we had received from previous clients.

Sensible proposals contain a section to describe the legal conditions governing the contract. These are written by lawyers to protect the company. They can be so legalistic that any prudent person would hand them to his or her own lawyers to check. The best that achieves is delay. We rewrote our legal conditions in language we could understand, words that would frighten no one. Then we played them back to our lawyer, to make sure the legal points were covered. By rewriting we arrived at conditions our clients thought fair and uncontroversial. They accepted them without hesitation; I remember only one legal argument in twenty-five years.

When you work abroad, you should say which legislation would be used in case of conflict, British or that of the country you are selling to.

Of course, it is best to present proposals in the language of the client, but only do that if a native speaker who understands your business writes it. The language must be perfect and so must the meaning. 'Quite good considering . . .' isn't good enough at all.

Remember our Swedish experience when we had a newsletter translated by Swedes who didn't know our business. They wrote nonsense.

Another detail: British companies, I have noticed, often quote and bill in sterling. That is easy and natural. I wonder if it isn't lazy too. We invariably billed in the local language and currency or, if we were unsure, in US dollars. Our aim was both to be courteous and to make it as easy as possible for clients to use us. It was for us to worry about exchange rates, not for them.

Though one proposal may seem like another, it is essential that it is not. To save time (who hasn't done this?) we'd sometimes take one proposal off the shelf, pencil out bits that didn't apply and add new words. Xerox was one company that saw through this short-cut and said so. It was a lasting lesson.

The brief

What many consultants – designers and all sorts – do is to take a brief, go away to fulfil it, then come back with the finished, considered answer. It is easy to see the reasoning behind that approach. The snag is, it doesn't always work. Clients may be disappointed, surprised even, by what they see. Important points may have been missed. Even if competent, the work may not fit the character of the company concerned. Matching the client's wishes as well as needs is not always easy.

When we started, my partner, an experienced designer, believed that the right way was to present the client with a complete and beautifully finished job. 'This', we'd say in effect, 'is the answer to your brief.' Beyond doubt, beyond peradventure. Coupled with this haughtiness was the fear that if we expressed doubt we'd lose face.

Now we'd all say this is arrogant nonsense. It is both wrong and risky to exclude the client from the process of arriving at a solution to what is, after all, his or her problem. Just as silly, most of the time, is the idea that there is only one solution to a problem. That shows a want of understanding as well as imagination.

The method we developed was more flexible, more modest – and a great deal more effective.

First, we'd spend a long time getting the brief right. Having spent days, usually weeks, reviewing the problem and elements bearing on it (future as well as current) we would draft the brief ourselves. Then we'd say: 'Is this what you have been telling us? Is this what you believe the problem to be? Have we understood it correctly?'

The reasons for doing that were threefold: we wanted to be sure we had understood; we wanted the client to be confident that they had said what they meant to say and that we had grasped the point. (How often do we assume that if we speak clearly the listener has understood.) And, while the best companies brief splendidly, others don't. We wanted to be sure we got a good brief, one that told us what we needed to know.

Partnership

Once we'd got the brief right and work started, we looked on the client very much as a partner in the project. We didn't disappear to any mountain eerie to commune among ourselves. In the course of almost every job, during which we were in constant touch, we would invite the client to what we described as a 'shirt-sleeve' session. We made it clear we were only half-way through the first phase of work. We had nothing finished to show or recommend. The client was invited not simply to monitor progress, to make sure we were on the right lines, but to advise us and guide us towards completion.

Apart from being immensely popular, that was sensible. For one thing, the client was involved in the process and felt part author of whatever came from it. He or she would be more likely to argue for it when the time came. For another, it stopped us working up blind alleys. From that early working meeting our efforts could focus more precisely on the right goals. The client, seeing all the rough workings and discarded ideas, was invariably astonished and reassured by the thoroughness of our approach – and by the value for money.

That attitude of working towards a solution with the client, of showing him or her all your early, unformed and probably poor ideas as well as those you think are better, isn't practised by everyone, but I recommend it. Peter Cree noted that in six years, out of twenty major programmes, only one design that grew this way was rejected at the formal presentation. That is a very high success rate.

While this approach seems reasonable when your client is near, people may worry that it doesn't make sense at a distance. Are you really supposed to bring clients from heaven knows where to show them unfinished work? Yes. It is true, in my experience, that they may be disappointed your work is so rough (they are used to seeing polished presentations), but only the first time. Once they grasp the partnership idea they are delighted. That is why it is most important to explain before people come.

Apart from its inherent sense, the 'shirt-sleeve' session is a great comforter to clients who hire consultants from abroad. You are far away. They must worry whether you have understood, whether you will do a good job. This gives them a chance to check before you present to the main board. That reduces their risk.

I don't say these working sessions should be thrown together. Though informal and relaxed, they should start with a restatement of the agreed brief, then show, one after another, the various lines of enquiry you have followed. Do show all the rough work. As well as comforting the client, someone in the client team may spot a gem among your rejects. That can happen, to everyone's delight.

In the same spirit, it is most useful to ask people in the client company how they want your work presented to the decision-makers. You don't have to agree. They will respect your experience too. When we presented finished work we always tried to describe the process we had been through, who had been involved, ideas we had rejected before we arrived at those being shown. Again, we presented alternatives, explaining the merits of each. It is a simple axiom of selling to offer choice. The choice should not be 'Do you like this or not?' but 'Which of these alternatives meets your brief best? . . . We recommend this solution because . . .'

What happens, as we've seen, is that clients can say 'fine, what happens now?' Rather than mumble that you will work out a programme of next steps, it is best to have them on the table in front of you. That both saves weeks and, once more, inspires confidence.

Super service

There is no point in peeling off platitudes about the need for good service. One statistic makes the point. For several years the revenue of my company grew by 70 per cent a year. That came, I dare say, because everything had clicked into place. Among other things, we undoubtedly sold well. But, here is the interesting fact: over two thirds of all our income came from 'repeat business'. Clients who used us one year came back to us the next and the next. That speaks not only for the quality of work we sustained, but also for the high level of service we provided. Excellent work with poor delivery would not have achieved those figures. In short, it is more than a courtesy and matter of pride and pleasure to anticipate and respond rapidly to a client's wishes, it is also good business.

Of course it is much more difficult to provide good service internationally than it is at home. I have said that clients in other countries are often afraid that suppliers or consultants coming from abroad will understand their needs less and be slower than local firms. This can discourage them from using you. It is essential, therefore, to overcome this natural concern.

Working late into the night, catching planes at first light, travelling in cold and wet and fog, waiting and snatching hurried meals by turn, making sure the client is kept delighted, day after day, that is the nature of servicing business abroad. In France, I'd been to see people in a large manufacturing group outside Paris. The meeting was chilly, not least because they were sure British service would be poor. That same afternoon others in my firm had also been to Paris. They had presented the last batch of sixty-three packages they had designed for Payot, the cosmetics firm. In four weeks our designers and studio people had taken multiple briefs, designed all those packages and working drawings in French, without a single mistake. The rush was to get Payot out of a jam. Few firms in the world, and none in France at that time, could have matched that service.

As I write I think with affection of the men and women in my firm who did so splendidly. As one American client put it, they 'always, unasked, went far beyond the call of duty'.

As well as a determination to excel, you need imagination to foresee what clients may want, even before they have thought of it. At one point we had a PR consultant, an old newspaperman. He was marvellous. We met weekly. Every time we decided to do something it was done at once. Gladly, I recommended him to a friend. They got on well, but drifted apart. I asked why. 'Oh, he is wonderful when I suggest what to do, but he has no initiative himself . . . he never phones me with an idea.' So good service means doing more than clients ask. You have to have their interests in mind all the time, looking for ideas to put to them.

Another lesson we learnt early: always double up. What happened was this: for years we worked for Tube Investments. We began, maybe, by designing a brochure. Then we created their corporate identity and applied it to seventy or more of their companies. Then we were introduced to their engineers in several manufacturing plants and we designed products for them (at least one won a Design Award). We made audio-visual programmes for their PR people. All very satisfactory. One day they came with another problem: TI had companies on the Continent and sold there, but few people had any idea of how big the group was. One year, for example, the rider who won the Tour de France did so on a Raleigh bicycle (a TI product), but no one in the group other than Raleigh gained any benefit from all the publicity.

TI decided to exhibit, a means of promotion more used abroad than in Britain. Our office in Brussels designed and erected one or two stands for them. But, it was easy to see, a comprehensive pro-gramme across Europe would be costly. In London we developed the idea of a modular exhibition stand, one that packed flat, could be moved easily, used and re-used. Trials were made at Olympia, then elsewhere. It worked, and it cut costs more than in half. It meant companies in the TI group would be able to exhibit in Milan, say, transport the stand to Zurich and re-erect it, then pack it flat again for Paris, very economically.

The head of corporate affairs, Bill Paterson, decided to introduce the scheme to companies throughout the group. Senior people came to London from all over Britain to a meeting. Then what happened? For the first and only time in his life, our man in charge of the project fainted as he got out of bed that morning. He never arrived for the meeting. Stupidly, he had decided to handle it alone; there was no one there to back him up. The TI people, who had come to London for nothing, were furious. Although, thanks to Bill's understanding, our other work for TI continued, that was the end of a most promising scheme.

There are two other points from that story. First, you saw how we had managed to sell differing services to various parts of the group. That was good. With it, though, goes the need to 'service in depth', as we put it. That is to say, when you meet a company you meet one person, or one or two people in the same department. It is risky to have one thin thread of contact with a firm. Liaising with just one person or one department makes you vulnerable. If that person goes, or if that one department finishes with you (even if they are happy with the work you have done for them), you are out.

There is something else. Often, you find that while the people you deal with can initiate and manage projects, others implement them. If they are not consulted, or want to be awkward, they can damage your success.

Often we surprised clients by wanting to visit as many of their plants and offices and branches as possible. We had two motives. One was to see for ourselves what the company was like away from its carpeted head office; we wanted to spot problems that might arise later and forestall them. Our second motive was to involve the staff, to hear their concerns and share our ideas.

This wish wasn't always appreciated; some clients thought it unnecessary. Standard Chartered Bank was one example. A fruit of the British Empire, the bank spread across India, Africa, the Far East, South America and, more recently, by acquisition, in parts of the United States. Some places knew it as the Chartered Bank. Others called it the Standard Bank. Bosses in London thought the time had come to have one global identity. At the selling stage, before they engaged us, we said we wanted to go and see. They didn't think it useful. We went anyway. One of us was in Singapore on business, so he took time to meet local managers. Another designer was in California on holiday. He visited the bank's branches there. A third was in India. When Peter Cree and others presented to the board Lord Barber, the chairman, said, 'You know more about us than you let on.' We won the job, but there were other benefits. Local people were delighted we'd taken the trouble to ask their opinion. One said, 'We don't know if we will like what you will do, but be sure we will do our best to make it work.'

We came to create a web of contacts throughout the companies we worked for, at various levels. That both reduces one's vulnerability and opens many door to future opportunity. We tried to match our service to the client's organization. Of course, sending several people to meetings where one would do is costly. We tried to 'piggy-back' – to combine non-fee-earning meetings with others where everyone was paid for. But even without that comfort, it is still best to work in teams. For one thing, your service becomes much better.

Often people in other countries expect more efficiency and better service than we, in Britain, are used to. Look at a Swiss train if you doubt it. The old delays and excuses that patch our delivery are not acceptable elsewhere. Nor should they be. It is my experience that working in other countries raises the standard of one's service at home. There's no question about it. So you become more competitive – and better – all round. That is the biggest bonus of all.

13 Harder Than It Looks: Acquisition

Cricket lovers remember W. G. Grace's advice: 'If you win the toss, ninety-nine times out of a hundred bat first. The hundredth time think about it, then bat first.' I'd say that about following any rules you set about acquisition. To grow internationally you may think about buying companies in other countries. I won't say, 'Ninety-nine times out of a hundred don't,' nor, 'Think about it then don't,' but I will say, 'Be careful.' The attractions are often illusory.

If you've got shares to trade or access to money, acquisition looks the easy way to move into other countries. At a stroke, or as soon as the ink is dry, you can have a ready-made company with clients, staff, know-how. You can bring something to them, to help them become even more successful. Further, you want to be more international, and so do they. It fits.

But wait: others have thought this before. Some have succeeded, many have not. In other words, while acquisition sounds sensible, straightforward, logical, it often leads to disappointment.

In my own field, I cannot think of a single firm which has not had its share of failures, including mine. Why is this? Are we notably less competent than anyone else? No. People in other activities have failed as often. We have had our successes too. Why is that? What did we do differently? Because there are so many variations, because every case is unlike another, it is hard to give firm guidelines for successful acquisition.

After we became a public company we made a number of acquisitions, eight or ten. Some worked triumphantly. Others were disasters. By and large, the companies we bought at home grew splendidly, acquisitions we made abroad were trouble. That is another warning. In time we became quite, perhaps very, good at making acquisitions in Britain, yet even with that experience we found foreign purchases more difficult. How will companies manage who have never done it before?

Looking at our own efforts, I think there are several keys. One is a paradox. In England we bought companies, mainly, to diversify.

From our design base, we moved into market research, then micro-electronics, then specialized financial services. We didn't know their field as well as they did, and never tried to tell them how to run their business. In one's own field, that temptation is hard to avoid.

I find it difficult to believe it is safer to buy a firm in a field you don't know than one in a field you do. But, unless you are stricter than we were, it seems to be so.

The way we paid for companies also prevented us interfering. Owners were expected to stay in the firm. Their main financial gain came from a share of their future earnings. That was a strong motivation, though it worked both ways. Once I criticized one company for something it was doing, in my view, badly. The boss, rightly, reprimanded me sharply. If he was responsible for profit and his wealth depended on it, I was not to interfere. Having said that, we were quick to help whenever help was asked for.

We worked only by friendship and persuasion, never by direction. There were three reasons for this. First, as we've seen, the basis of our acquisition was that people were rewarded for their own effort. Any interference might, in their eyes, have jeopardized that. Second, we had taken great pains to find good companies and good people. It seemed absurd to me to second-guess them. Third, when people sell their companies they are afraid they will be told what to do. This is debilitating. It destroys enthusiasm and initiative. We tried hard not to do that. We wanted to earn goodwill, so that people would come to feel that being part of our group was good for them.

I have little time for acquisitions based solely on the bottom-line. That's a cheerless way to live. From the centre of the group we produced leads for operating companies, helped with PR and in other ways. We encouraged one company to help another. But it was always voluntary. We worked to build a sense of partnership, of everyone aiming at common goals. It worked to the extent that after three years as a public company a fifth of our clients were using the services of more than one practice area.

So what about acquisitions which failed, or disappointed? I think of the United States, graveyard of so many hopes, but others too. Our experience falls into two parts: learning, and forgetting what we'd learnt.

Our early days, in Norway, Sweden, Belgium, have been described. You will have drawn your own conclusions. Mine would include:

1 Making mistakes about people.

2 Under-investing.

3 Expecting results too soon.

4 Interfering.

5 Thinking ownership brings control.

No doubt it is harder to assess people from other countries and cultures. This implies no criticism; it works all ways. In one case we 'inherited' a man and knowingly ran the risk. In another, I ignored local advice. Today I would take more care.

Under-investing matters for another reason. Some companies wanting to work abroad don't have limitless funds; they need to be careful. I think now you can be too careful. 'There must be a meaner way' is the watchword of so much official and business life in Britain that I come to think prudence is a weakness. The danger is that if you don't invest enough, local people will be daunted by unnecessary difficulties, and so turn in other directions for their income.

On the other hand, if we spend more we want quicker results. That's risky too. As Jan Stael von Holstein pointed out, we expect much quicker results from abroad than ever we would at home.

The practical route to successful acquisition in other countries is first, to invest enough to attract and keep good people. That is expensive, particularly when you add in all sorts of hidden costs you may not be aware of. Second, sustain support for a long time. Third, do not attempt to acquire until you can afford your (high) estimate of first, second and third year costs. One qualitative research company we helped start broke even after nine months and made a profit thereafter. Its budget was to break even after two years. But that was thanks to Sue Robson, one of the best in England. Sue is exceptional. The general rule is to expect to take twice as long as anyone says in his or her first enthusiasm. Companies fail both because they don't earn enough revenue and because they earn more than they can fund. Overtrading kills companies as surely as undertrading. That is why pessimism is needed in the first place and continued commitment is vital in the second.

I have already talked about not interfering. But when does friendly support become interference? Answer: when the person at the other end thinks it does. But, if you clone yourself in another country, isn't it right that you should strive for common standards and ways of working? I'm not sure. We saw how Bill Goodenough succeeded in Singapore by working to a fixed price, which we wouldn't have countenanced in England. While his method necessarily differed, Bill's quality was and is excellent. Perhaps that is a larger point for companies wanting to acquire companies in other countries.

Years ago, we formed a jointly owned marketing consultancy company with John Kerridge, now the brilliantly successful chairman of Fisons. In my ignorance, I pressed for more than 50 per cent of the shares. To my surprise, John agreed at once. 'Why?' I asked him later. 'Because,' he replied, 'I'm running the company and I know I'll control it.' And he was in the same building as me.

To suppose ownership brings control can be misleading. People on the spot run the business, whatever owners abroad like to think. The essential point is not only to recognize that and to let them, but to encourage them to want to run it the way you do. That takes time and may, once more, be considered interference.

There's the paradox again. You know a lot about your own business. You might easily be ahead of the firm you acquire. Should you impose your methods? We tried that. In one case I remember saying, 'We've done it your way. It hasn't worked. Now let's try our way.' But that didn't always work either.

Why not? Christopher Lorenz, who manages the management page in the *Financial Times*, once described how companies try to copy the methods 3M use to develop new products. They fail, he said, because they adopt the method but not the culture. If you put your own boss in place that helps; indeed, the way to instil your methods is to have people from the acquired company spend enough time in your offices to come to prefer your way.

Acquisition is not the only route. If you are satisfied with the quality of the firm you look at, other ways of working together could suit you better, as our experience in France showed. Philippe Rasquinet, a man who'd been with us in London for ten years, started his own office with three thoroughly experienced partners. Their quality was beyond question. Philippe, at home with our methods, used them. We tried to fund the company or have shares in it, but Philippe's partners weren't keen. So we made a franchising arrangement. We provided case histories, help when asked for, and our name, in exchange for a small percentage of his revenue. The arrangement worked splendidly.

When we went public and knew we would want to make bigger acquisitions, we wrote down some criteria. I believe we succeeded when we followed them and failed when we forgot. To go back to W. G. Grace, the excitement of the moment can so easily overwhelm you that it is vital to stick to whatever rules you write. These were the notes we made:

Acquisition criteria and notes

1 Purpose

- To reinforce or broaden our existing services either in the UK or abroad.
- To broaden the services and financial base of the group.
- To add profits.
- To improve P/E (the profits/earnings ratio, whereby financial analysts rate the performance of companies).

2 Criteria

- Activity to *fall within our area of competence* (managing high quality services).
- Activity to be *attractive to our existing customer profile* (services – or products? – of value to senior management).
- Activity to be *capable of growth*, on its own; with capital; or with management.
- Activity to be capable of *above average rate of return* in its field.
- Level of investment of time and money to be *affordable* easily.
- Profit contribution to suit group goals. Specifically, we should not depreciate short-term profit for the sake of long-term revenue. [I disagree emphatically with this now, but that is what we wrote then.]

3 Questions to ask

3.1 *Activity*

- Is the company within our framework (high quality creative and management services)?
- Do we understand it?
- Is there any synergy?

3.2 *Market(s)*

- Does it serve the same client profile as we do?
- Does it bring new markets we'd like?

- Size of their market?
- Is it growing?

3.3 Strength in market

- Share?
- Reputation for: quality, service, price?

3.4 Competition

- Now?
- To be expected?

3.5 What is necessary to succeed in that business and market?

- Quality?
- Reputation?
- Fast service?
- Low price?
- Volume?
- Distribution?
- Unique offer?
- How does the company rate?
- What are its shortcomings?
- Would we strengthen its ability to compete? How?

3.6 Management

- How good – intelligent, industrious, organized?
- How efficient?
- How deep? Is 'succession' good?
- Is it marketing oriented?
- Is it technically oriented?
- Would we get on well?
- How would we relate to them – through one profit centre, more than one, board only?

3.7 Finance

- Is there strong asset backing?

- In their industry is their rate of return above average, average, below average?
- Do they 'plough back' profits?
- Do they keep a reserve?
- What is their return on investment?
- Would they need funding?
- Will they agree our accounting rules?
- Would we be expected to do their accounting?
- Is there potential for more profit from their existing activity?

3.8 Potential

- How much will they grow themselves?
- How do they plan to do so?
- Could we help their growth: with capital injection, with management, in some other way?

3.9 Risk

- To our cash?
- To our reputation?
- To our management time?
- Could we contain the risk?
- What would be the effect on our resources, our cash flow, and over what period?
- Could we borrow money needed? At what cost? With what effect on our gearing ratio?

3.10 Draft forecast of benefits

- Finance: first year, second year, third year?
- Client base?
- International?
- Management skill?
- Other?

3.11 How should we pay?

- Cash?
- Shares?

- Part cash, part shares?
- Loan?
- Joint venture?
- Would we seek *all* shares, over 50 per cent, under 50 per cent?

These criteria were drawn up some time ago. How would you strengthen them? Today I would change quite a lot, notably the insistence on short-term profit at the expense of long-term revenue. And I would place far more emphasis on the calibre of the people who will actually run the business.

We bought good companies when we did that. We made poor acquisitions when we focused excessively on finance as, of course, accountants and merchant bankers, the people who manage your acquisitions, do. They lose good deals because they can be absurdly precise about the wrong things, like five-year cash-flow forecasts which they and everyone know must be invented. They even juggle these made-up figures to make them look better. Once satisfied, they can recommend acquisitions which will never work because the people are wrong. The marriage will never work.

The idea that money conquers all is the biggest myth. On this subject, as on so many others, the Romans were nearer the mark when they said, 'Love conquers all.' If not love, then genuine friendship, partnership, caring, helping, supporting, encouraging.

People run companies. Plans and promises don't. People are the key to successful acquisition. But often, notably in a service business, you buy from founders who want to leave before long. You may think, and they will say, that all they care about is the amount they are offered. Mostly, they don't mean it. For one thing, if they are good, they will care about the future of the staff. For another, it is their baby they are parting with. At some moment, the emotional impact of that will hit them with overwhelming force. Money then becomes meaningless.

I was lucky to learn that before we went public. Maurice Saatchi of Saatchi and Saatchi wanted to buy us. Martin Sorrell, who has built WPP from a firm making wire plastic baskets for supermarkets into the world's largest advertising agency by a process of acquisition, was there too, as Maurice's finance director. With some reluctance I agreed terms. Maurice met the people in my firm and satisfied them. Then Maurice's accountants used some pretext about our accounts to reduce the offer. Meanwhile my heart had grown heavier by the day.

The financial point was a try-on. Both Maurice and Martin have since said they should have bought us. They would agree that it is short-sighted to be too clever; it is much better sense to be generous. You win rather than lose. Extra money is soon recouped if you buy a good company and the people in it are strongly motivated. A lot of people had put a lot of effort into building what we had. I hated the idea of deserting them. That taught us at first hand the power of the emotions. In all our early acquisitions we consciously addressed them. Monty White, our financial director, would hold the talks about money. I looked after the emotional side of the people we bought from; I understood what they felt and meant what I said.

At a loftier level, the story is told of how Lord Forte of Trust-House Forte bought the George V, the Plaza Athenee and La Tremoille, three grand hotels in Paris. He had heard that the owner had it in mind to sell them. He went to Paris to see her. She put off the meeting. A secretary regretted she was indisposed. Most of us would have left Paris in a fury. Not Lord Forte. He sent her a bunch of roses and hoped she'd recover soon. A day or two later he phoned her. He bought the hotels, it is said, over breakfast.

So the emotions of the founders can be decisive. There is a second refinement: although the founders may remain influential, it is wise to look at the executives below them. If there is no succession, you probably shouldn't buy. Often the next generation has been in the shadow of the founders. The main reason for our string of successful acquisitions was that we took the lid off the top of the company, creating the second generation. We let them rip, as they had always wanted to rip. Almost without exception, these younger people in the companies we bought were wonderful. Their departments or companies took off, each month better than the one before.

We did not replace one boss (the founder) with another (us). We cared about a few things, but mostly tried to encourage and support the staff. Quite quickly people saw they were not threatened and responded well. I dwell on these 'post-acquisition relations' because they make or break any purchase. The easy bit is buying a firm. The hard part is to let it flower with the spirit, and in the context, of your own company.

What do you do when things go wrong? As this book has noted already, that's the test. I talked of being prepared to have faith and to give support for longer than you expect. But you also see good parent companies dragged down by the continuing failure of an overseas subsidiary.

Easy to say, it is a question of deciding why the firm is not prospering. One research company we had in New York never did move, and it never would under the man in charge. We knew that, but continued to have faith. We'd go often to try to help, and always found an increasingly listless environment. In that case, the right thing to do was either to put in our own boss quickly, or to close or sell the company.

Another company we had in the US makes the point still more strongly. My successors bought a company which started to lose money. Rather than stop the drain, they spent more and more on it. They did send their own accountant, but that wasn't enough. In no time, good companies in England were sold to pay for the American drain. In less than three years they had to sell the whole group. Away from the problems, it is easy to say, 'Cut off failures. Swallow your pride. Forget what people may say,' including the stock exchange, which should be pleased when you are resolute.

To end on a more constructive note, let me touch on a most successful acquisition. The case is puzzling because it seems to break the rules anyone would write. So why did this work? For a long time I wanted my firm to move into the micro-electronics industry. Though our product designers understood and used micro-electronics and the head of one of our market-research companies was computer crazy (he had nine at home), as a company we knew little about the industry. Certainly I was and am ignorant. I had two reasons for wanting to enter the industry. First, it struck me as the biggest and most influential growth business for the rest of this century. If we weren't in it, we'd be out of it, not understanding a mainstream of commercial life. Second, various parts of our business used computers and they would gain by knowing more about them. There was some synergy.

I looked for over a year, met many firms, and worried about the keys to success in that field. Coming back from Australia, I sat next to a professor of micro-electronics from Hamburg University. I asked him, as I had others, this question: 'There are 500 micro-electronic consultancy companies in Britain today. People say in five years time there will be fifty. What will make those fifty survive?'

'Look for three things,' my German acquaintance advised. 'First, companies that are close to their customers. Second, people who can adapt their technology rapidly. Third, firms that manage their money well.'

The firm we bought was outstanding at the first two. We knew it and had employed it in the past to help our product designers. The company was owned mainly by outside interests, though the director had shares too. It was a micro-electronics consultancy company that worked largely for water boards, adapting US products to suit the special needs of the water industry.

When Monty White, our financial director, and I visited the company we spent a morning being bemused and dazzled by one piece of equipment after another. It was all Greek to Monty and me. After lunch we asked the principal, David Viewing, what he would do with any money we brought him. Prepared for the question, he filled the blackboard with hieroglyphics. From behind the blue smoke of his cigar, Monty burst out laughing. 'It is obvious', he said, 'that you know as much about money as we know about micro-electronics. We should get on famously.' We did – but not straight away.

After that agreeable day David sent me one of the rudest letters I have ever received. On no account would he part with the business, least of all to us. We were all sorts of awful things. Happily, we recognized the outburst for what it was: shades of having one's baby snatched away. I wrote to David, then went to see him. Being the generous man he is, David saw beyond his nervousness. We became the firmest of friends and I believe he and his colleagues enjoyed our association. We bought the company from David's majority shareholders. That first year it lost £70,000. Four years later David's company was valued at £5 million – another example of a clever man bursting forward when his previous owners left.

That was a successful acquisition from every point-of-view. Some clues suggest why. First, we took great care to think what we were looking for, no doubt doubly so because we were ignorant of the industry. David Viewing's fledgling company had demonstrated it was close to its customers and did adapt its technology rapidly. His was a consultancy business, so we weren't in the dark quite as much as I imply. Second, we were confident we could provide the financial controls we needed. Third, we were lucky. David Viewing is not far from being a genius. He combines high technical knowledge with great imagination and a powerful drive. Credit for success goes to him, Andy Faulkner and others in his team. Fourth, we honoured his independence. We saw ourselves as there to enable him, to give him the support and encouragement he needed. We put up funds for him to develop his own product, for instance, and set up his financial systems. We helped him with PR (I remember spending a weekend thinking of a name for his product – Husky), designed his brochures, helped arrange sales meetings, but only when he wanted us to. It was his firm. We were lucky to be involved with it.

That was our attitude to acquisition.

14 Summary

You have read how one service company, based in London, built an international business with dozens, even hundreds, of friendly, satisfied clients around the world. You have been relieved to see there has been no picture painted of omnipotent and relentless success. Quite the reverse. You have been told of plenty of errors, accidents and silly mistakes, for three reasons. First, in my view we learn more from things that go wrong. Second, I have tried to be truthful (and checked everything I can with people in the firm at the time). Third, perhaps the main message is that building a business anywhere is difficult and working abroad doubly so.

None the less, our main line of advance was sound. Results say we must have been doing something right. The aim and hope of this book is that you will take time to jot down how *you* would have managed things – whether much the same or in other ways.

Pulling it all together, what is there to learn?

Doing business internationally is no longer an option. Everywhere is now an international market. Look in your local shop window if you doubt that. The competition we have to face at home comes from Korea no less than Kettering, Boston and Bremen as much as Birmingham. Nor can you dig a hole and hope the fierce winds from across the Channel will blow over your head. One safeguard, of course, is to focus on so-called 'niche' businesses, and I agree with that. But even then you are not secure. The American consultants Arthur D. Little wrote that occupying a niche is only safe while no one notices it. Once you are rumbled, the effect of international competition, they said, can be like a steamroller flattening a road.

Thus the prime reason for developing international competence is to protect yourself at home. Because we work in an international arena, our clients have access to the best manufacturers, suppliers and consultants in the world. Every advance – of computers, electronic communications and the rest – adds to that truth. Beating the world's best is the new game, one that will last as long as business lasts.

Even in the domestic market, you read how my firm repeatedly won work in Britain because clients liked our international experience. That gave us a competitive advantage over some of our British competitors. I have also noted that to succeed abroad you have to meet expectations of performance which may differ from those you are used to. Perhaps the main benefit of working in other countries is the way it drives up one's standards. That stands you in good stead everywhere.

As you saw, we had another defensive reason for building business abroad: we didn't want all our eggs in one basket. Relying wholly on the prosperity of one country is risky. Up to a point, that strategy worked for us. Yet as our international revenue grew, year on year, so did that from the UK. Try as we did to widen the gap, nearly three-quarters of our work came from companies in Britain. Still, to have a sizeable share of our revenue coming from elsewhere was a comfort.

Another advantage of working abroad is that good staff want that experience. They know how important, stimulating and often enjoyable it can be. International experience both adds to their knowledge and helps provide job satisfaction. To attract and keep good people, think internationally.

So much for defence. What about being more assertive?

There is scarcely any need to point out the infinite opportunity open to very many companies of all sizes. Everyone knows it is there. As the European Community develops, the challenge will be inescapable, yet many find the prospect daunting.

George Formby sang a song:

> If women like them like men like those
> Why don't women like me?

That is a tortuous way of saying that our competitors abroad may be no better than we are, or not as good. We should find out. Perhaps, if we shape ourselves properly, we have a chance to beat them. What you need to succeed internationally is the same as you need here: to care about your customers, your products (or services) and your people. To focus on your customers, take pains to find what they want and more pains to provide it with superb service. Those are universal keys.

While doing all that abroad is more difficult, the principles are the same. Many of the skills you possess already are transferable. There is comfort in this. It means more firms can compete abroad than might think so. However, there is an obvious qualification. Your competence has to be expressed in new ways, perhaps with more flexibility and adaptability too. We have to give our clients or customers in other countries what *they* want, the way they want it, not (as occurs often at home) what *we* want in ways we want.

So there are new skills to acquire. Through the stuttering progress described in this book you can see what some of them are. My hope is that you can avoid some of our struggles and move forward faster. Perhaps I have not given enough time to strategic considerations, though they are stated. One reason is that your time and place is different from ours. You will need to evolve your own strategy.

Our horizons, you will recall, were initially no wider than northern Europe. We started small, being sure we could afford our inevitable mistakes. We backed off when we feared we couldn't. That prudence continued. Though our aim was to spread risk, by offering a range of services to a range of industries in a number of countries, we started one at a time. Germany was our goal, though we said we would only go there when we were ready. We were clear where we would commit effort and money and where we would not. That, very simply, was our strategy. Later it grew. We felt it was time to invest in the United States, the world's largest market. More modestly, but as purposefully, we started a company in the Pacific basin, which we looked on as 'the golden tomorrow'.

What your strategy should be I cannot say, except that you need one. People mock when I talk of military principles, but they apply — focus, concentration, having the right equipment and resources, sustained back-up, continuing training and the rest. We worked once for a biscuit manufacturer who proudly boasted their goods were sold in sixty-seven countries. They collected export markets like stamps, each with the same, slight value. That is no way.

When it comes to international business, there is everything to learn from the Japanese. They take infinite care to decide which markets to penetrate and how to do it. They know more about competitors they'll face than the competitors do. They come in with a strategy to win. Significantly, they do not look for instant returns. It is a market share they want.

Without realizing it wholly, that was our aim too. We wanted to become an international business and be recognized as one. Ours was a long-term view, one I would advocate. Unless your position is exceptional, I do not believe you can build a sustained international business by expecting quick returns.

But something else comes first. It lights your path, underscores every decision you take. That is vision. You have to start with a *vision* of your company as you would like it to be some years ahead. Once when I used that word a friend said, 'Oh, that's the same as planning. We do that already.' It isn't. The vision precedes the plan. My view is that the prudent people in business today, sensitive to the world about them, will want to see their company as an international one. That is quite different from being a local, or British, firm that exports a bit and would like to do more. If you say, 'Yes, we ought to do more abroad,' this book can help you. But if you continue to see yours as a domestic company whose main concerns are confined to Britain, you will fall short of both the challenge and the opportunity of our time.

The real plea of this book is for an international vision which touches and informs all you do. With it you will develop products or services to beat international competition which you know well. You will train yourself and everyone else in your company to serve clients or customers in other countries as naturally as they would the big buyer down the road. Should you resolve to become international in mind, and follow the consequences patiently, spreading your vision to everyone, you will create a different – and more competitive – company. There is security for all in that.

Appendix: Useful Contacts

In addition to your professional institution or trade association and the British embassy or consulate in the cities that interest you, the following organizations may be of help.

Association of British Chambers of Commerce

Sovereign House
212A Shaftesbury Avenue
London WC2H 8EW
Tel: 071–240 5831/6

Local chambers of commerce provide practical help, advice and courses to members on many aspects of exporting; the association can put you in touch with the chamber in your area.

Association of International Courier and Express Services

PO Box 10
Leatherhead
Surrey KT22 0HT
Tel: 037–284 2953

British Exporters Association

16 Dartmouth Street
London SW1H 9BL
Tel: 071–222 5419

Export houses perform a variety of functions, including acting as agents. Most specialize in particular markets, and the association can give full details.

Business in the Community

227A City Road
London EC1
Tel: 071–253 3716

Business Statistics Office

Government Buildings
Cardiff Road
Newport
Gwent NP9 1XG
Tel: 0633 815696

A central agency which monitors businesses in the manufacturing, service, distribution, energy and mining sectors, and has links with the European Community.

Central Office of Information

Hercules Road
London SE1 7DU
Tel: 071–928 2345

The COI may be able to help you publicize your services overseas.

Centre for Information on Language Teaching and Research

Regent's College
Inner Circle
Regent's Park
London NW1 4NS
Tel: 071–486 8221

Chartered Institute of Marketing

Moor Hall
Cookham
Maidenhead
Berkshire SL6 9QH
Tel: 06285 24922

Courses, publications and advice for members on all aspects of marketing.

Chartered Society of Designers

29 Bedford Square
London WC1
Tel: 071–631 1510

Confederation of British Industry

Centre Point
103 New Oxford Street
London WC1A 1DU
Tel: 071–379 7400

An independent organization of industrial and commercial companies and associations which offers members extensive information and advice on all aspects of running a business.

Defence Export Services Organisation

Room 707
Stuart House
23–25 Soho Square
London W1V 5JF
Tel: 071–632 4826

DESO is part of the Ministry of Defence and helps British firms sell their defence products and services overseas.

Department of Trade and Industry

19 Victoria Street
London SW1H 0ET
Tel: 071–215 7877

The Enterprise Initiative is the Department of Trade and Industry's comprehensive self-help package for British business, providing advice, contacts and, in some cases, funding for the use of consultants across a wide range of areas. The Export Initiative is of particular interest to businesses trying to penetrate overseas markets, and is administered for the DTI by the British Overseas Trade Board.

Regional DTI offices

North East
Stanegate House
2 Groat Market
Newcastle upon Tyne NE1 1YN
Tel: 091–232 4722

Cleveland Office
Tel: 0642 23220

North West
Sunley Tower
Piccadilly Plaza
Manchester M1 4BA
Tel: 061–838 5000

Liverpool Office
Graeme House
Derby Square
Liverpool L2 7UP
Tel: 051–224 6300

Crewe Office
Tel: 0270 500706

Preston Office
Tel: 0772 653000

Kendall Office
Tel: 0539 723067

Yorkshire and Humberside
25 Queen Street
Leeds LS1 2TW
Tel: 0532 443171

Hull Office
Tel: 0482 465741

Sheffield Office
Tel: 0742 729849

East Midlands
Severns House
20 Middle Pavement
Nottingham NG1 7DW
Tel: 0602 506181

Derby Office
Tel: 0332 290487

Chesterfield Office
Tel: 0246 239905

Leicester Office
Tel: 0533 531245

Lincoln Office
Tel: 0522 512002

Northampton Office
Tel: 0604 21051 ext. 35

West Midlands
Ladywood House
Stephenson Street
Birmingham B2 4DT
Tel: 021–631 6181

Stoke-on-Trent Office
Tel: 0782 285171

Droitwich Office
Tel: 0905 794056

Telford Office
Tel: 0952 290422

South West
The Pithay
Bristol BS1 2PB
Tel: (0272) 272666

South East (London)
Bridge Place
88–89 Eccleston Square
London SW1V 1PT
Tel: 071–215 0574

Reading Office
40 Caversham Road
Reading
Berkshire RG1 7EB
Tel: 0734 395600

Reigate Office
Douglas House
London Road
Reigate
Surrey RH2 9QP
Tel: 0737 226900

Portsmouth Office
Tel: 0705 294111

Margate Office
Tel: 0843 290511

Chatham Office
Tel: 0634 828688

East
Westbrook Centre
Milton Road
Cambridge CB4 1YG
Tel: 0223 461939

Norwich Office
Tel: 0603 761294

Ipswich Office
Tel: 0473 212313

Chelmsford Office
Tel: 0245 492385

Scotland
Scottish Export Office
Industry Department for Scotland
Alhambra House
45 Waterloo Street
Glasgow G2 6AT
Tel: 041–242 5495

Wales
Welsh Office Industry Department
New Crown Building
Cathays Park
Cardiff CF1 3NQ
Tel: 0222 825097/823258

Northern Ireland
Industrial Development Board
Export Development Branch
Marketing Development Division
IDB House
64 Chichester Street
Belfast BT1 4JX
Tel: 0232 233233

For advice on specific markets you can go direct to the contact points
listed below:

Western Europe: 071–215 5336

Eastern Europe
General: 071–215 5258
USSR: 071–215 4257/5265
Czechoslovakia, GDR, Romania and Yugoslavia: 071–215 5152/5267
Albania, Bulgaria, Hungary, Mongolia and Poland:
071–215 4734/5

North America
Industrial goods: 071–215 4608/4563
Medical and scientific goods: 071–215 4563
Consumer goods: 071–215 4593/4595

Latin America, Caribbean and Australasia
Brazil: 071–215 5050
Argentina, Chile, Paraguay and Uruguay: 071–215 5059
Bolivia, Colombia, Ecuador, Peru and Venezuela: 071–215 5286
Mexico and Central America: 071–215 5291/5290
Caribbean: 071–215 5297
Australia: 071–215 5319/5321
New Zealand, Papua New Guinea, the Pacific Islands:
071–215 4760/4759

Middle East
Arabian Gulf: 071–215 4246/5239
Israel: 071–215 4949
North Africa: 071–215 4947/4948
Other Middle East countries: 071–215 4366/5314

Sub-Saharan Africa
East Africa: 071–215 5226
Anglophone West Africa: 071–215 4970
Francophone Africa: 071–215 4971
Southern Africa 071–215 5011

South Asia and Far East
Japan: 071–215 4804/4805
South Korea: 071–215 4747/4808/4758
Indo-China, North Korea: 071–215 4736
Burma, Indonesia: 071–215 4738/4741
Singapore, Malaysia, Brunei: 071–215 5143
Thailand, the Philippines: 071–215 5253/5489
Pakistan, Bangladesh, Nepal: 071–215 4821/4824
Taiwan: 071–215 4729
India, Sri Lanka: 071–215 4825

China and Hong Kong
China: 071–215 5357/4827
Hong Kong: 071–215 4848/4829

The Design Council

28 Haymarket
London SW1Y 4SU
Tel: 071–839 8000

European Commission

rue de la Loi 200
1049 Brussels
Tel: 010 322 2351111

European Community Economic and Social Committee

2 rue Ravenstein
1000 Brussels
Tel: 010 322 5123920

European Investment Bank

100 bd Konrad Adenauer
2950 Luxembourg
Tel: 010 352 43791

69 Pall Mall
London SW1Y 5ES
Tel: 071–839 3351

The bank finances capital investment in industry, energy and infrastructure which help European integration.

The Export Buying Offices Association

c/o Portman Ltd
360 Oxford Street
London W1A 4BY
Tel: 071–493 8141

EXBO is an association of the London buying offices of leading overseas department stores and importers. It can advise manufacturers on the suitability of their goods for foreign markets.

Export Intelligence Service

Export Opportunities Ltd
Export House
Wembley Hill Road
Wembley
Middlesex HA9 8BU
Tel: 081–900 1313

Export Licences

The Enquiry Unit
Export Control Organisation
Room 540
Kingsgate House
66–74 Victoria Street
London SW1E 6SW
Tel: 071–215 8070

Export Market Information Centre

1 Victoria Street
London SW1H 0ET
Tel: 071–215 5444/5

Export Marketing Research Scheme

The Association of British Chambers of Commerce
4 Westwood House
Westwood Business Park
Coventry CV4 8HS
Tel: 0203 694484

Export Publications Unit (DTI)

Lime Grove
Eastcote
Ruislip
Middlesex HA4 8SE
Tel: 081–866 8771

Fairs and Promotions Branch (DTI)

Dean Bradley House
Horseferry Road
London SW1P 2AG
Tel: 071–276 2414

Financial Times Profile Business Information

Sunbury House
79 Staines Road West
Sunbury-on-Thames TW16 7AH
Tel: 0932 761444

Freight Forwarders

British International Freight Association
Redfern House
Browells Lane
Feltham
Middlesex TW13 7EP
Tel: 081–844 2266

Harmonised System (HS) Classification

HM Customs and Excise
Dorset House
Stamford Street
London SE1 9PS
Tel: 071–620 1313

Institute of Export

Export House
64 Clifton House
London EC2A 4HB
Tel: 071–247 9812

A professional body devoted to the development of UK exports, and
providing courses and seminars on exporting.

The International Chamber of Commerce

ICC United Kingdom
Centre Point
103 New Oxford Street
London WC1A 1QB
Tel: 071–240 5558

Language Export (LX) Centres

Co-ordinating Unit
Regent's College
Inner Circle
Regent's Park
London NW1 4NS
Tel: 071–224 3748

London Enterprise Agency

4 Snow Hill
London EC1A 2BS
Tel: 071–236 3000

Enterprise agencies provide business advice, counselling and training. For the address of your local agency, phone Business in the Community on 071–253 3716 or, in Scotland, Scottish Business in the Community on 031 5569761.

The London Enterprise Agency organizes the London Export Enterprise Programme with support from the Department of Trade and Industry and Lloyds Bank. A part-time course over six months, it aims to help small businesses establish their potential in overseas markets and devise an effective export plan through a combination of practical training, syndicate work and counselling. The programme takes place in London, but is open to businesses trading anywhere in the UK.

Market Research Society

15 Northburgh Street
London EC1V 0AH
Tel: 071–490 4911

Professional body offering courses, seminars and a wide range of publications on market research.

Resource

1–3 Birdcage Walk
London SW1H 9JH
Tel: 071–222 5373

Sponsored by the government and BSI, Resource aims to promote technical co-operation in key overseas markets in the fields of standards, quality assurance, metrology and testing.

The Simpler Trade Procedures Board (SITPRO)

Venture House
29 Glasshouse Street
London W1R 5RG
Tel: 071–287 5751

Small Firms Service (Department of Employment)

Offers information and advice to new and established firms on how to build a successful and sound business and on how to access new markets. The Small Firms Service operates through Small Firms Centres which can be contacted by dialling 100 and asking for Freefone Enterprise.

Statistics and Market Intelligence Library

1 Victoria Street
London SW1H 0ET
Tel: 071–215 5444/5

The DTI's comprehensive collection of foreign statistics, trade directories, development plans and other published information on overseas markets. Free access to personal callers; short enquiries can be dealt with by telephone.

Technical Help to Exporters (DTI)

Linford Wood
Milton Keynes MK14 6LE
Tel: 0908 220022

Index